Divine Confinement

Facing seasons of limitation

BRENDA A. SMITH

**Executive
Books**

Divine Confinement

Published by
Executive Books
206 West Allen Street
Mechanicsburg, PA 17055

ISBN: 0-937539-87-2

LCCN: 2005931825

Cover Design by Jeff Horch

Printed in the United States of America

This book is dedicated to:

Heather Richardson who daily
demonstrates dependence on God

Meredith Hurd who consistently
acknowledges God's realities

Jeff Horch who relentlessly grasps
the grace of God

Fred Smith, Sr. whose forever love
is the best ever support net

Mary Alice Smith whose blessing for me
is to make my life count

CONTENTS

WORDS OF GRATITUDE

"You know who I really respect?" Dad's question certainly had my full attention. "I respect Moms who write books while their children nap." The challenge was on the kitchen table. So, even with a young corporate husband, graduate school courses and two children under age two I had my marching orders. It didn't take long to recognize that respect would have to take a different turn. Thirty five years later I sat late at night and wrote what the Lord put in my heart about the care of dying parents. Suddenly it dawned on me that we had come full circle. I reminded Dad of his visit so many years ago and ended by simply saying, "I wrote a book—while you slept."

The men and women who courageously shared their stories bring life to this book. Their wisdom, humor, humility and perseverance continuously teach me about what God can do in and through those who are given wholly to Him. To them I am deeply grateful.

As a prodigious reader I have always loved reading the words that express thanks. Despite a variety of styles the bottom line message is the same—writing a book is a team project. In scripture we are told over and over that the furtherance of the Gospel requires a multiplicity of gifts and efforts.

Reminiscent of award ceremonies there is "no way to thank everyone." But I want you to know about some who are fellow travelers. Thank you to my brother, Fred Smith, Jr. and sister, Mary Helen Noland who believe in and pray for me. "Would you read this and give me your thoughts?" became the prelude to confinement for a most special group of friends known as The Sisterhood: Chris Miller, Lana Lombardi and Marlisa Mills. Their objectivity and listening ear smoothed the rough places and lightened the load.

Ron and Lily Glosser, Steve Brown, Charlie "Tremendous" Jones, and Dave Nelson encouraged me to hold the course. Johanna Fisher, Pat Walters, Lynda Goellner and Vicki Hitzges challenged me to keep my eyes focused on the Lord.

My children and grandchildren create an atmosphere of love and trust that make desiring God a top priority. Thank you Bob, Heather and Andrew Richardson; Brian, Meredith, Colby, Caden and Colin Hurd; and Jeff Horch. Your faithfulness in your own confinements shows me that we serve a living and true God. A special thank you to

Jeff whose indefatigable technical support, straightforward thinking and clear vision kept this project moving and above all, focused. I have deep gratitude for your confidence that God's grace is foundational and that we serve a powerful, sovereign Lord.

There would be no book without the lives of Fred Smith, Sr. and Mary Alice Smith. Their love, their encouragement, their hope, their suffering and their example of faithfulness have changed my life.

And all glory to the Lord Jesus Christ without Whom there would be no story. May Jesus Christ Be Praised. Laus Deo.

FIRST WORDS

We are beginning a journey together. You have picked up this book because you are in a time of confinement, or someone you love is. You have felt that gut-wrenching sensation of having your feet slip on life's icy patches and you want some answers. I want us to think about what confinement is. I want us to see that confinement by God's design is purposeful and intentional. And then I want to share with you principles that I have drawn from a lifetime of experience, in career, mothering, marriage and divorce, as well as managing the care of two aging parents. In this book they are called The Five Footholds. They are guidelines for successfully facing seasons of limitation and confinement. I thank God for His relentless hold on us. When our feet are awash in the muddiness of our circumstances He grips us with an everlasting grasp.

A Community of Care

My own experience quickly broadened into dozens of interviews with men and women throughout North America about their times and seasons. It was clear that we all grow for the benefit of others. The quilt of human existence is colored with squares contributed by each one of us. Perhaps my story brightens the corner for someone else. And your story brings color and texture to the entire piece. The life quilt encompasses a saga of faithfulness, courage and perseverance. There are strands of laughter and threads of tears. Thankfully the common denominator is God's divine purpose. We are formed as a fellowship of faith to display His goodness. We are not alone in our times of confinement. Please remember that the Footholds are your work to do, but they are done in community. You are sewing your square but it will enhance the entire quilt. For years I struggled with the notion that my square had better be perfect "or else." As a recovering perfectionist I am more forgiving of myself and others when I see errant stitches and slightly mismatched shadings. The stories that you will read are of real life, flesh and blood people who struggle with choices, consequences and circumstances. They are creating something beautiful because God is in it. They will introduce you to confinement, its sorrow and its joy, so that together we may rejoice.

Pigs and Pythons

Ken Dychtwald, PhD in his ground-breaking book on demographics calls the generation between 40 and 60 the "pig going through the python." This startling picture is drawn from the bump in the post-war America birthrate. The long thin line is brashly interrupted by an enormous swell and then settles back down…thus, the pig in the python. What does this have to do with confinement? EVERYTHING. The boomers have driven our economic development for the last 50+ years. This group changed the face of marketing for whatever they did drove the demand. This generation is now pioneering the "sandwich generation" experience. For the first time more than 80% of all Americans will live past 65. This aging phenomenon predicts millions who will know the confinement of care—both receiving and giving. Women, in particular, will share the support of parents, children and grandchildren. Confinement is certain. The life lessons that we learn today in our tough places will better prepare us for those that are to come. As a young Mother I had no idea what was ahead, but my awareness that "life has rules" has made each stage somewhat easier to navigate.

One of my goals for this book is to help you successfully make it through life's transitions. If you are in that "boomer bulge" you know the challenges of career, parenting, health and relationships. You know what it feels like to be stuck. The time pressures of your life clearly define what living in a box feels like. During this time I want to help you learn lessons that will serve you well for the rest of your life. Another goal is to strengthen and encourage those who, like me, are into the later phases. Much to my surprise I suddenly became "the older woman" of Titus 2. No time for whining and complaining—this is a rich opportunity to offer my scars, my scares, my kneelings and my reelings to you. You may be balancing career and caregiving or you may be receiving support from those who love you dearly. It is often difficult to share your emotions with those closest to you. I hope to be a voice for you. My third goal is to see the eternality of God's truths revealed and revered. Remember that what He is teaching us is timeless. Unlike cartons of milk, there is no freshness stamp on His wisdom.

Communion in Confinement

"They sang a hymn and went out to the Mount of Olives" is the introduction to one of history's greatest confinements. And thank God, it was indeed a divine confinement. Jesus was leading the disciples to the Garden of Gethsemane. Little did they know what lay ahead, but no detail was overlooked. Jesus was preparing for physical, emotional and spiritual confinement that would release us from the bondage of sin. The Father was satisfied with the acceptable sacrifice of the Son. And the disciples would begin a season focusing on their challenge "to be satisfied with what satisfies God," in the words of Lewis Sperry Chafer. Little did they know when they sang that hymn and went out how their world had irreversibly changed.

Martin Luther told us: "Next to the Word of God, music deserves the highest praise. The gift of language combined with the gift of song was given to man that he should proclaim the Word of God through music." Many dark nights have been brightened by the singing of familiar hymns learned in childhood, or powerful choruses written by anointed contemporary musicians. I would encourage you to ask God to bring music to your mind as you read and as you apply the Footholds. Remember, "They sang a hymn."

The singing of the hymn was more than ritual for the disciples. It was responsive. They were participating together and sharing a very personal experience in the upper room. As I wrote I prayed that the illustrations would resonate with you. I want you to catch your breath and stop for a minute thinking about your own life story. Just as the disciples shared this upper room experience together so we can share our lives with each other.

Could Jesus have been more vulnerable and transparent than He was in Gethsemane? As He knelt and pleaded with His Father He was exposed to the betrayal of Judas and the militia's capture. In order to do God's work in this world we must risk betrayal and capture, as well. Included in the text are entries from my caregiving journal. They are used with the prayer that the raw emotions expressed in the writings will touch a place in your heart. They are shared as my response to an intense experience, but not a unique one. Many women are wondering and wandering in the process of providing care for those whom they love. And many more women will be given that privilege in years to come. My cries to God are an admission of my own weakness and His glorious power. It is my own point of suffering and accession to "Thy Will Be Done."

The Process of Reading

Tim Sanders in his fantastic book, *Love Is The Killer App* recommends that reading should be an interactive process. He marks key ideas and summarizes big thoughts. I also think that reading should spur questioning. As thought prodders I have added summaries and questions at the end of the Five Footholds. They are for personal consideration as well as group discussions. For me, prayer is one of the most profound ways of responding to God. I have provided a space at the end of each Foothold for your own private moment with the Lord. In high school I had a prayer journal in which I would earnestly pour out my spiritual struggles. However, it was written in pencil so that I could erase it regularly. That way I was protected from my Mom's being privy to the tribulations of the teenage years. This book is yours—this space is for your devotional thoughts. Be as real with Him as He is with you. And write in pen!

Throughout the pages of Divine Confinement you will find the words of men and women who know both the character of God and the nature of man. Their adeptness at thinking and writing stirs my soul. I want you to benefit from their wisdom and their work so I have listed books that may offer further insight. The bibliography doesn't begin to scratch the surface, but these suggestions may help you in your journey.

There are ideas that permanently mark us and people who write with indelible ink on our lives. For example, Fred Smith, Sr.—my Dad. He is certainly a man of character and integrity, but more than anything else, he is a man who loves me. To know me is to know him. Throughout this book you will hear his words and feel his influence. Rather than reference him formally, I choose to simply say, "My Dad." Undoubtedly you will benefit from his wisdom as have I. Undeniably you will see ink stains throughout these pages. I have been so very blessed and it is only fitting that you should be, too.

Encouragement

Recognizing that God is with us and that He loves us through anything and everything has changed my life. My feet still slip and I continue to be threatened by stumbling, but He is reliable. He truly is the "I am that I am God in my it is what it is" situation. When He showers me with His abundant grace I am free to ask for help and then be of help.

My prayer is that you will find confidence in the dependability of God. My desire is that you will be enlivened, encouraged and energized to see God's hand of intention and purpose. My hope is that you will know Him more deeply. And my anticipation is that together we will sing a hymn and go out to embrace our Divine Confinements.

"To everything there is a season and a time to every purpose and a time to every purpose under the heaven."
Ecclesiastes 3:1 (New International Version)

"All I have needed thy Hand hath provided, great is Thy faithfulness, Lord, unto me."
Thomas O. Chisholm

1

CONFINEMENT WITH A PURPOSE

The oysters of ordinary life create the pearls of eternity

Do you ever feel like you are under house arrest? You aren't locked in a prison cell, but you are severely restricted in your movement. Your heart is constricted, your physical world is reduced, your vision of the future is narrowed, your ability to function is minimized…all share the common nature of limitation.

Is the wonderful experience of home schooling requiring changes in your lifestyle? Does your manager expect you to be in the office, always on call when you know that your productivity is enhanced outside the office? Did your choice to return to college alter your career path? Do your family obligations narrow your geographical choices? Have the consequences of a decision taken away your liberty? Are your ailing and aging parents living with you and your family? Is your abusive spouse creating marital bondage and fear for you and your children? Have you decided that you are too old to accomplish your dream? Has a physical disability taken away mobility? Are your financial straits diminishing your options?

Yes? Then you understand confinement.

Confinement is a very old word that came into popular usage to describe the postpartum period of "lying-in" prescribed for all new mothers in the 1930s and 40s. They were kept in bed for no less than 7 days to recover their strength. The word now describes everything from a straightjacket to incarceration. It conjures up visions of imprisonment and the removal of rights. Americans espouse the Western song philosophy of "don't fence me in," so seasons of limitation are not warmly received.

15

On Sundays our family would faithfully attend the First Baptist Church of Ft. Thomas, Kentucky—a 20 mile one-way drive to cross the Ohio River and enter true Southern Baptist Convention land. Mom's Sunday best always included hat, heels, gloves….and a girdle. Without fail we would attend services, go "out to lunch" and then head home. No sooner had we hit the door than Mom would scurry down the hall, close their bedroom door and make a most familiar sound—"AHHHHHHHHHHHHHHHH!" The sound of Amazing Grace in the service was no more familiar to us than this afternoon sigh of relief. My Mom had taken off her girdle and we all experienced her freedom from confinement.

Lock Up is a Let Down

Elvis romanticized life in legal confinement with his "Jailhouse Rock." But we intuitively know better. The reality of imprisonment is built into the sounds of our culture. Johnny Cash touched nerves with "Folsom Blues." The television series Law and Order runs an ad campaign based on the distinctive electronic sound that signals the beginning of the show. "What is that sound?" the ad asks. Apparently, it is the sound of our justice system at work. Years ago Dragnet closed with a heavily muscled, profusely sweating arm pounding a hammer. The sound was instantly recognizable. But the clank of metal door hitting metal jamb is chilling to all of us. This says that freedom is on the other side.

Martha Stewart became a pop icon for confinement in 2004. A comment was made that house arrest on 153 acres defies logic. For in fact, the electronic tracking equipment's range is less than the square footage of her house. She remarked during her five months of imprisonment that she exercised regularly, avoided fatty prison foods and even cooked pasta for her cocaine dealer roommate. But she was noticeably relieved as she embraced her family warmly upon release. Even the most lighthearted remark about "involuntary sabbatical" rings rather hollow in the light of reality.

Do you get inklings of the purposeful and intentional nature of this confinement? Have you started to recognize life lessons that may have come no other way? Are you learning that perfectionism is a "chasing after the wind?" Is your heart strangely warmed by the awareness of God's grace? Has he built a boat around you in the storm? Does the opportunity come to share comfort with others in similar circumstances?

Yes? Then you understand divine confinement.

What is the difference between confinement and divine confinement? The world views confinement as anything that stifles your activity, your dream, your options or your individual freedom. But divine confinement in its simplest form is recognizing that the hand of a loving and sovereign God has ordained a season of limitation for His glory and our good. *The oysters of ordinary life create the pearls of eternity.*

Charles Haddon Spurgeon in his sermon, *"The Hairs of Your Head Numbered"* has a defining word about confinement: "Everything is in the Divine purpose, and has been ordered by Divine wisdom. All the events of your life—the great, certainly; and the smaller, with equal certainty. Our happiness lays very much in our complete submission to the Lord our God. Oh, it is a blessed thing when we know that God is ordering all the events of Providence. Then we dissolve our own will into the sweetness of His will and our sorrow is at an end! Since even the very hairs of our head are all numbered; since everything is really ordained by the Most High concerning His people, let us rejoice in the Divine appointment, and take all as it comes, and praise His name, whether our allotment is rough or smooth, bitter or sweet."

How have others faced these seasons?

When our feet are slipping on ice or we are scaling the face of a mountain-sized life experience we need footholds that will provide traction and stability. Facing these seasons of limitation by finding in Him surefootedness will enable you to turn a prison into a learning lab. These grippers will provide not only stability but forward motion. Just getting out of the slide isn't enough. It is important to stop the spin and keep moving toward the goal. These principles allow you to shift from marking off days on the cell wall to expectantly looking for the lessons. When I was a child my parents told me repeatedly that I could go kicking and screaming or I could go enthusiastically. Either way I was going to go! Seasons of limitation are much the same way. They are inevitable just as natural seasons come and go. The key is to travel well through these times. In the following pages you will be introduced to the Five Footholds for Seasons of Limitation. They will provide the "tiger paws" needed to maintain your footing.

God's Intentionality

David, the shepherd King, repeatedly spoke of nearly falling but being rescued by Jehovah. As a shepherd he was keenly aware of the rough terrain and the importance of balance. In many ways he was limited as he tended to the care of his father's flock. I imagine that he didn't have many hours to kick back and just enjoy the great outdoors. But think of what he learned during those times! His expert eye-hand coordination was developed as he warded off the threats of wild animals. If he could lead sheep, he was certainly equipped for the strong-willed people of God. These seasons give us a structured learning environment that prepares us for future use. David's life foundation was built on tending and fending. What is God doing in your seasons of limitation?

Gertrude (Biddy) Chambers was a sickly child who missed winter months of school and eventually dropped out to help her Mother. David McCasland, in his biography of her husband, Oswald, observes: "While other children might have languished in self-pity, young Gertrude was not deterred by her winter confinement and lack of formal education. She had a single ambition—to become secretary to the Prime Minister of England. So she set herself to studying Pitman's Shorthand at home and learning to type." There are few confinements more divine! In mastering these skills she was preparing herself to transcribe every sermon, every lesson, every meditation and spend the 49 years after her dear husband's death producing "the books," as she called them. There were over 50, in addition to leaflets and booklets. In 1935 *My Utmost For His Highest* was published and is now an internally-recognized devotional classic. My Mom and Dad thoroughly exhausted five copies of the little red book in their 67 years of marriage and daily readings. Biddy's confinement served as the instrument of God's kind, purposeful blessing.

Why think about divine confinement?

If you are between the ages of 40 and 65 you are fondly thought of as the "sandwich generation." Carol Abaya coined this wonderful phrase to describe the experience of meeting the needs of both aging parents and growing children. Although I intuitively disliked being a pile of corned beef I took on the identification until I recognized that *I am a "rock and roll woman"*—rocking my grandchildren and rolling my parents. This was a hilarious realization sparked by a random comment in the drugstore. "Why do you have both Depends and Pampers in your basket?" "Because I am a rock and roll woman" was my spontaneous response.

Your life may not be touched by caregiving whatsoever. Your confinement may be defined by job stress, relationship difficulties, health issues or being a stay at home Mom. But everything that you learn will be woven into the next experience. Life is not a series of unrelated events but an intertwining of lessons learned and practiced. As I look back over my life I see that in each confinement I intuitively established traction. But it was trial and error…sometimes much error produced by much trial. I want to organize the principles that I have learned in order to help you survive and thrive throughout each season of confinement.

Today is Preparation for Tomorrow

I want you to know that where you are today is not only where God can meet you and grow you, but where you will be refined for the next step. Learn well because the boxes get more interesting as you age—and as those around you grow older. As a "rock and roll woman" I finally get to be a star on Dick Clark's American Bandstand! He never ages but all of us who longed for fame and fortune in Philly are definitely on the right hand side of the aging curve. We want you to see us doing this right because we want you to give us some excellent care when it is your turn to care. If you are approaching your 40s, 50s or 60s, statistically you, too, will be a rock and roll woman. By 2007 39 million Americans will be actively involved in caregiving. 75% of these will be women. Just as we don't come to parenting with an instruction manual, we are often left on our own as caregivers. Taking a prospective view of life will make this time more valuable, more productive and more enjoyable. Look at your confinement and see how God is schooling you for the future. In his divine economy no moment is ever wasted.

A business friend of my Dad's had a handwritten sign on his wall, "Having done my best today makes it easier to do better tomorrow." I would modify that to say, "Having learned God's lesson today makes it easier to apply it tomorrow." Your divine confinements will teach you about yourself, about God and about His plan for your life. And do not worry about practice time—He will faithfully provide.

What is the value of a Divine Confinement?

In 1998 my life was full and fulfilling. I was an officer with a major insurance company working with stimulating people and doing rewarding work. My home in Iowa was the Hotel Fort Des Moines allowing me to live out my fantasy of being Eloise at the Plaza. However, visits back to Dallas pointed out that my parents were noticeably feebler. It was time to come home. In the early months of 1999 I moved back and began slowly assuming the role of care manager. Without knowing it, serious confinements, both personal and professional, had been working to prepare me for these next years. And new seasons were opening that brought unexpected joy, unfathomable pain and unmistakable views of the goodness of God. Let me share a few key seasons with you and outline the lessons that were being branded on my soul and my psyche. Stop along the way and think of where you are and what lessons you are learning.

Seasons of Life

I think I first identify limitation as a young mother. In a moment of crazed enthusiasm I applied to Vanderbilt University to pursue a Master's degree. We had one child less than six months old, one car and lived in an apartment miles from the campus. My on one semester, off one worked well. By the time I received my graduate degree I was the mother of two daughters under the age of three and pregnant with son Jeff. No doubt that I was busy. But I felt devoid of options, even when I had chosen the very circumstances that limited my freedom. Seasons are not always disastrous, nor dangerous. They can be filled with happy chaos, but they still create boxes. During this time I began to learn the value of a support network. My church, my friends and the world's greatest babysitter allowed me to stop the roller skates just short of the cliff many hectic afternoons. My Mom, Mary Alice, would sense that the laundry was exploding out of the laundry room and intriguing bowls in the refrigerator were forerunners of the science projects soon to grow on deep dark back shelves. At just the critical moment she would announce her arrival, grab an apron, hoist a child onto her hip and make sense out of incredible nonsense. She earned her Mary Poppins title!

Small Spaces—Big Graces

1971 presented very real challenges. My husband moved us west of Pagosa Springs, Colorado for four months. There were five of us in a 10x48 mobile home. Without water, TV, radio, or phone this actually was more accurately seen as a trailer. For all the things that we didn't have we were replete with mice. During one of Mom's Mary Poppins excursions she reached into the sink and came up with a very bloated and very dead mouse. The concept of shock and awe started that day in Pagosa Springs.

The hallmark of this adventure was arriving and noticing the unmistakable odor of a decaying animal. My husband opened the refrigerator door and was greeted by the head of a black bear, left by the former occupant well before the electricity was shut off. Arguably the grizzly took the prize for true confinement, but we suffered right along with him!

Many of our seasons fade into obscurity. This one is permanently tattooed on my memory. But I learned that there is no situation in which you cannot find good—and in which you cannot find God. It was during this time that I acquired a spiritual hunger beyond all natural bounds. God met me in that trailer and taught me of His faithfulness, his sustaining grace and my identity in Him.

Reality Check

The era of "super Mom" resulted in a season of hospitalization that gave me understanding of physical incapacity. After a serious bout of pleurisy and pneumonia I was checking out of the hospital when a doctor stopped by to say, "As I saw them rolling you in I assumed you would die quickly." I learned that trying to be all things to all people was foolishness with a high price tag. He pointedly brought home the principle that perfectionism isn't only irresponsible, but that it is sin. One of the greatest constrictions for me is lack of physical strength. The tension between what I want to do and what I can do is a lifelong struggle. Acknowledging the reality of limited energy has been an ego struggle. The comments that I make later on about perfectionism are first person. They were patiently taught by a loving God and not so patiently received by me. Self-protectionism and control were held in a tightly closed fist. He had to unclasp my clenched fingers and it hurt! But what joy He restored in removing what I was hoarding. Peter speaks of doing God's work through God's strength. I learned the exhilaration of know that "when I am weak, then He is strong." I began to understand that with His grace I could handle all that He hands me. "Were it not for grace is now my anthem."

Transitions

1986 marked the end of a 20 year marriage. Even through an extended separation and excruciating marital deterioration the Lord built into my heart the fundamentals of what are in this book as the Five Footholds For Facing Seasons of Limitation. First of all, I had no place to go but to Him. Dependence on my own strategies proved thoroughly worthless and undependable. But He, indeed, proved worthy and dependable. Learning to see, accept and live in the light of reality was developed through the unswerving counsel of friends and family. "Denial is not a river in Egypt" was plastered all over me. The tighter the box became, the more I ran from the truth. The Lord kindly, but firmly, showed me what His truth was. He was ever the "I am that I am God in an it is what it is situation." It took years, but that box has now been redeemed and recycled as an altar to His loving kindness. Months of eating disorders and aimlessness showed me that my God-given safety net was woven with human hands that held strong. Truly, without the steadfastness of family, church friends and co-workers I would have drowned in self-pity and irrational behavior. Nearly twenty years later I am the older and hopefully wiser woman who wants to be used in the comforting of others. I am walking everyday in thanksgiving and a desire to make my life count. I write this for you as an encouragement, as preparation and as a safe place to think about dark times and lonely places. He has turned my cells into celebrations. The joy in my heart is as real as the despair of earlier years. When He unlocks the door it is time to fly.

The most wrenching confinement was a separation from a precious daughter subsequent to the divorce. Four years of relational breakdown taught me that the Lord has a purpose for the most perplexing and painful times. During this time I watched a movie about a family with a son in drug rehab. The mother and son were estranged. She tearfully said, "I wasn't ready for him to go." My heart broke. When a child is born you prepare for their departure in 18 years, but a premature break creates a cavernous hole. I stared at the TV, began sobbing and cried out repeatedly, "I wasn't ready for her to go!" This was a season of confinement that still touches me deeply. Today "the years that the locusts have eaten" are being magnificently repaired and gladly restored.

Caregiving

It is against this backdrop of limitations and learnings that the most intense season is being played out…a season of caregiving.

By 2000 it was clear that a change for Mom and Dad was coming. Their declining health was making it difficult to maintain high quality, independent living. Meals deteriorated, medications were randomly administered and it was time to consider alternative living arrangements. For 18 months I planned, talked with my brother Fred and sister Mary Helen. I spent hours drawing up ways of modifying my house and even started dreaming about it. When I broached the subject informally with Dad he smiled and said, "Dreaming about it means that you have moved it deep into your subconscious. I appreciate that, but your Mother and I are just fine."

Throughout this time Fred, Mary Helen and I met regularly to consider future alternatives. At the time my sister was teaching third grade at Trinity Christian Academy in Addison, Texas. At our first confab we sat in elementary sized chairs around a tiny table discussing very adult issues. The irony of the picture was not lost on us. This was the first of many planning sessions. If you are in this process spend time solidifying your thinking, your expectations, your action steps and your options. Don't assume anything. Our family has been blessed with closeness and yet we found the next months trying as we ironed out the who, what, why and how much of Mom and Dad's care.

A wonderful family dinner at a favorite restaurant gave us the opportunity to present our proposed plan. I would modify my home to create a separate suite for Mom and Dad. With the assistance of Ofelia, our daytime home health care assistant, we could produce a homey environment that would give both privacy and protection. Being totally project oriented I jumped into the reconstruction knowing that this would be the best of all worlds for them. January 15, 2001 was moving day. For weeks before the entire family had packed, unpacked, piled, unpiled and finally garage saled. As they moved in it felt somewhat like "The Night Before Christmas," but instead of stockings' being carefully hung we had pictures, memorabilia and familiar things all diligently hung with great care. Every attempt was made to transform their suite into the place of happy memories, past, present, and future. They moved in with acceptance, appreciation and an attitude of blessing. We were heading into a season with great expectations and no instructions.

Learning Environment

Remember the powerfully enigmatic opening line of *Tale of Two Cities?* "It was the best of times; it was the worst of times." How appropriate for this season. Together we have experienced triumphs of the human soul and the depravities of the human spirit. So many wonderful lessons are being learned. Sometimes I don't see it until God has thoroughly "schooled" me. God has given Mom, Dad and me precious moments of insight and understanding that we would never have known without the experience of living together. Early in this season I had an amazing "AHA!" For nearly 15 years I had lived by myself and actually thought that great maturity had occurred. In fact, I prided myself on the giant steps I had taken. Within weeks of their move-in I realized with a jolt that I was still the same, selfish woman. It just had not shown up when I lived by myself. It is easy to be mature all by yourself!

But in all of this we are growing. I have been pushed to come clean on the impact of stress on my life. Admission of my own human failing has opened a door to embracing the grace of God. Caregiving, like all other periods of confinement, brings our productive strengths to light, as well as our destructive weaknesses. It may not be my only season of confinement, but it is one that is working on me most stringently.

We have endured life threatening hospitalizations, agonizing rehabilitation and debilitating disease. Mom has gone to heaven and Dad has faced death four times in three years. During the long nights I have rejoiced, rejected and repented—repeatedly. I have laughed, cried and looked for meaning...sometimes simultaneously. As many do, I turned to casual journaling as catharsis and release of the emotions. They are lightly named Musings and Amusings About Caregiving. As you know I am sharing several of the entries with you throughout the book in order to demonstrate that 1) it is perfectly normal to need a place to scream 2) God is big enough, strong enough and faithful enough to hear our tormented cries 3) Love finds its way through the torture and remerges brighter and shinier 4) In each and every season of life we are being equipped for the next step 5) There is joy in the journey when we see God's plan and God's hand.

Redemption

Redeeming the time is foundational to all confinements. How do we make the most of where we are? How do we come through stronger? How do we use our experiences for the benefit of others? Answers to these questions are critical during these seasons. A good example of using the time to best advantage is www.breakfastwithfred.com. We have created an online archive that allows us to relevantly communicate the lifework of my Dad. A dear friend called one day with a pointed question: "How are you going to keep from wasting this time?" My initial offense turned into an outline as I realized that the hours of physical containment make this season of confinement a divine gift from God. A sense of purpose moves us toward redemption. Unfortunately, we often kick against the divine design of our confinement. God has designed a season that is perfect for me—I must only rest in Him and accept its architectural features. No more remodeling of the season—I am going to live where He ordains.

The movie theme song asks the probing question, "What's it all about, Alfie?" How I understand the depth of that question. What it is about is learning to depend on God, not casually, but wholeheartedly. Through this comes an understanding of freedom in limitation. The paradox of giving myself to God only to be given back has begun to solidify in my brain and in my heart. I am grabbing hold to His grace because it is the only place I can put my slipping feet. Wherever you are you may be feeling that you are stuck. You may be moaning about the lack of life and options. You may well be asking what it is all about. Stop and see that your whining may be blocking your view. Accept that this confinement is yours—uniquely yours—designed by a loving God who knows exactly what you need at this moment to repair and prepare. Take a long look at your life and take the long perspective. Wherever you are is a training ground for the work that has your name on it. And, if you live long enough you will be able to share the fellowship of care…either as giver or receiver.

Purposeful Confinement

I want you to embrace the concept that He confines to refine that we may shine. When we come out "shining like gold" we will show forth His glory. As you take this journey step by step I want you to be strengthened in the Spirit. I want you to consider your life and the seasons of limitation that the Lord graciously has ordained just for you. May the Lord bless you in your confinement. May His divine design encourage you, conform you and make you useful for the Kingdom.

Confinement? Of course, but thank the Lord it is Divine Confinement.

MUSINGS & AMUSINGS

"Moving Day"

"Where was I when we moved?" "How did you get all these things in here?" Simple questions, but repeated over and over. The decision was made that it was time for Mom and Dad to live with me. We made flawlessly detailed plans. We wove a grand story of "the new place and the better life." The big day finally came and we carefully moved Mom before the truck arrived to prevent the sadness of seeing the empty house. Sounds logical and rational—but it became a tangle of yarn thoughts too knotted to untie. How could she be sitting in her old familiar chair one moment and then sitting in a new chair in a new place the next? Where did the house go? My fairy tale geriatric center was accessorized with all of their belongings and memorabilia. But I left out the critical process of connecting the dots. The almost-clinical way of providing a better quality of life dismissed the importance of our messier emotions. I can take her back to the house, but her things are gone. I can walk her around the new rooms and point out everything, but it "isn't home." Dad gently tries to settle her mind, "wherever I am is home, sport." But she will certainly ask again and again, "How did I get here?" She didn't get to say goodbye.

MUSINGS & AMUSINGS

"Divine Confinement"

"You must feel confined." Just a passing comment but it scored a direct hit in my soul. Confinement, yes that is exactly what I feel. I am under house arrest. I sit in my office and look out the window much like Robert Louis Stevenson lay in a childhood bed of sickness and pretended grand and glorious adventures. Sadly, I often go into an electronic stupor and overdose on HGTV. But this isn't a random confinement – this is one appointed by God—this is divine confinement. I can either continue making chalk marks on the wall denoting time served, or I can see that this is really a learning lab created to mold me into usefulness. Haven't I been confined before—a really bad marriage, a broken relationship with a child, a job with no hope of success, an addiction to chocolate and ice cream, a mean and jealous spirit, a wandering heart—aren't these all confinements? But how much better to see God's hand in this and know that He has the key and that He came to set the prisoners free. I won't be here one day longer than I need to be and in an ironic twist Mom and Dad won't be here one day longer than God knows that I need them to be. Who is taking care of whom? Aren't they the stuff of which this confinement is made, so aren't they the stuff of which the divine purpose will be constructed? And then, ultimately they will be my source of freedom for I will learn to trust Him, love them more dearly and understand freedom is not lack of confinement, but the recognition that it is divine.

Five Footholds For Seasons of Limitation

- **DEPEND ON GOD**
- **ACKNOWLEDGE THE REALITY**
- **GRASP GOD'S GRACE**
- **WORK WITH A NET...WORK**
- **MAKE IT COUNT**

"For when I am weak, then I am strong—the less I have, the more I depend on Him."
(2 Corinthians 12:10 The Living Bible)

"Nothing in my hand I bring, simply to Thy Cross I cling."
Augustus Montague Toplady

2

DEPEND ON GOD

Without Him we can do nothing;
within Him there is nothing that we can't do.

We sat at the conference table in his office overlooking a large metropolitan area. He had agreed to discuss the first outline for *Divine Confinement*. I was armed with all my interview questions. However before I could start he made the comment, "You missed a principle." Quickly, I responded, "Which one?" "The first one—dependence." "Oh, that will be the foundation of each chapter. It will be woven throughout." "No, if you don't start with that you aren't being honest with the reader or yourself." Thus began a penetrating discussion that created Foothold Number One —Depend on God.

Our inadequacy and His sufficiency

When he was busily building a thriving business he realized that in his own strength he could not be the husband that he wanted to be. Appropriating God's sufficiency was the next step. He made the decision to consciously turn off work as he stepped out the back door into the parking lot and do nothing but pray for his wife until he arrived home. The result was a marriage and spiritual partnership with far-reaching impact. "It was easy for me to see my inadequacy. The harder part was understanding the complete sufficiency of God. *"Learning human inadequacy is the first lesson, but unless you grab hold of total dependence on God, the lesson is incomplete."* Hunger for Bible study and prayer deepened the growth process. Challenges further broke down the human adequacy and built up the sufficiency of Christ for him. One of the most severe lessons occurred in 2003. His wife fought the good fight with cancer and went home to be with her Lord and Savior. "I thought that I had been broken before, but this season is like no other." He is walking through deep sorrow and profoundly understanding that without Him, we can do nothing; but within Him there is nothing that we can't do.

Independence versus dependence should not be the issue for Christians; it is our inadequacy versus His sufficiency. Our challenge is to move from I can to I can't to He can! When we believe that we are able, we are unable to receive the blessing. As JI Packer says, "Christians deprive themselves of their most solid comforts by their unbelief and forgetfulness of God's promises." Margaret and Don suffered the traumatic murder of a precious child. It was a random senseless shooting that turned a young husband into a grieving widower. Just hours before a joyful phone call had announced the news of a move back home. Now their daughter was dead. How could they possibly survive? "We knew we were out of control. We knew that our human coping skills were totally inadequate. He carried us; He lifted us up and over the horror and put us on the other side." They had lived out the promise "I will never leave you nor forsake you." Hebrews 13:5 (New International Version)

God knows best

When my daughter Meredith started talking she would refuse help by loudly asserting, "Myfelf! I'll do it myfelf!" When we face difficult seasons we want to think that we are capable of mustering up the resolve, the energy, the competence, the experience, the stability, the enthusiasm—the whatever it takes to handle it. "I won't bother God with this one—I will wait until the going gets really rough," was the way one woman put it.

Chris Miller is a potter in South Florida. The work of her hands is closely aligned with the work in her heart—the touch of God. She opens my eyes to life's everyday truths by showing me lessons of the clay. In thinking about self-sufficiency she said, "We are always so quick to say we can do it, and then we jump in head first, fail, and wonder what happened. It's like firing the clay for the first time. I have a kiln with a computer on it. I set the computer for a slow-rising fire, thinking that the rise will be slow enough for all the moisture to evaporate out of the clay and come out in one piece. If the firing is too fast, the clay pieces can explode. I was having a lot of explosion problems. So I started this thing called candelling. It's when you put your pieces in the kiln, and set the kiln on low for a long period of time. This prepares the clay for the higher firing later. JUST LIKE IN REAL LIFE: God prepares us for those higher fires by putting us in lower fires for a longer period of time. We cry and complain about it . . . but if we got our way, we would be blown into a million pieces. God knows best."

The provision of His resources

In seasons of limitation not only our circumstances create boundaries but also the finiteness of our resources. The bottomless cup of coffee doesn't exist in the human condition. The sucking sound of emptiness will come eventually. Gloriously, the death rattle of personal adequacy is the opening chorus of God's sufficiency. Our American culture says "fake it until you make it." Or "don't ever let them see you sweat." It is all about image. Too often our heart wants to write the story of the conquering hero. On my bulletin board is an old cartoon from the New Yorker magazine featuring three business associates seated at a bar. The one dejectedly holds his drink and says, "So far, I've been a survivor, but, of course, I used to think I would be a dominator." For Christians victory is in prevailing on His grace, not prevailing over our circumstances.

Recognizing that where we are is by His hand we start to understand that we have no resources that He hasn't provided. There is no "Myfelf!" Accepting this can sometimes be different from knowing, realizing or understanding it. The great hymn, Great is Thy Faithfulness has an intriguing line: "All I have needed, Thy Hand hath provided." When going through one of my life's most painful confinements I walked each morning, singing those words over and over. One day it suddenly dawned on me that this meant my very circumstances of suffering were divinely designed, provided and needful. Could this be true? J.C. Philpot indicates that the answer is clearly yes: "It is a great and inestimable mercy when our various trials and troubles are a means of driving us to the Lord, as our only hope and help. Those circumstances, outward or inward, temporal or spiritual, which...stir up an earnest spirit of prayer, make us cease from the creature, beat us out of all false refuges, wean us from the world, show us the vileness and deceitfulness of our hearts, lead us up to Jesus, and make Him near, dear, and precious—must be considered blessings."

In discussing confinements Sandra smiled and said, "I thought that I was born with the 'happy gene.' One of my strengths was always the fact that I wasn't moody—I was always the one that brought the sunshine in—or at least I didn't rain on anyone. But a mysterious undiagnosable illness changed all of that. My good mood was from Him—I wasn't as sufficient as I thought. It came as quite a shock to know that what I thought was my core personality was nothing more than a gift from the Lord. I was truly inadequate. I think that I lived as a 30/70 Christian. I would do my 30%; He would do the rest. I would get 30% of the glory and He got the rest. After all, it was the supermajority of the credit's going to Him! But now I know that is all of Him and none of me."

Clinging to the Cross

"Bend down and hear my prayer, O Lord, and answer me, for I am in deep trouble." (Psalm 86:1 The Living Bible) Caroline was in an abusive marriage, but managed to put on the face of a highly-paid professional woman. She operated as a key executive and no one knew that when she went home she "was in deep trouble." Years of fear; years of mistreatment; years of dreading tragedy for herself and her children—these finally drove her to flee with only what she had in her hands. The woman's shelter became home and a new beginning. But how would she tell her boss? How could she expose them to the imminent danger of a homicidal husband? What would happen to her? The Lord truly bent down and heard her prayer. He opened the door for a favorable hearing and an overwhelming response of love and protection from her co-workers. She began her step by step journey toward safety. She followed the tread of the Savior and He led her. Now she leads a group of recovering men and women who have said "Enough." I cannot do this alone. I am helpless but You are my hope. I am homeless but You are my refuge. I am weak but You are my strength. At her baptism she spoke of the faithfulness of God and the love of His people. She was in deep trouble and God bent to hear and answer.

My friend Johanna Fisher teaches me daily about depending on God. She instructs me wordlessly about His dependability. We share the experience of caring for aging Moms and seeing them go home to glory. One morning these words formed in her mind: "I am clinging to the Cross of Christ and holding on for dear life." That is exactly what she is doing. He is sufficient because His death was acceptable to God. He paid the price for our sin. He can be depended on because He was deemed worthy. She is holding on for dear life because she is inadequate. No, she isn't incompetent. In fact, her years of service to KCBI, a Christian radio station, have given her a place of distinction in the Dallas-Fort Worth metroplex. She is articulate, poised and capable. But, she is dependent on Him for every breath. She is holding on for dear life. The spiritual says it this way, "It's me, it's me, Oh, Lord…Standing in the need of prayer."

His faithfulness in our darkness

"Congratulations, it's a boy!" Their decade-long struggle for parenthood had finally ended. Their decades-long struggle of parenting a disabled child had just begun. "What strengthens you?" "First, he is our gift from God. We have been given everything that we will need to be Jamie's Mom and Dad. But more importantly, we have a God who is never surprised by even the darkest moment. If we thought we were in this alone we would be distraught, but there is not a step that we take that He hasn't gone ahead of us." Humanly we are incapable of managing such deep water but divinely the waters part and God makes a way.

Charity's eyes welled up with tears as she talked of God's care. She related a story of emotional abuse, fear and finally release. As she unpeeled the onion of her confinement I was holding my breath. "What kept you sane and safe?" "God's love and protection," was her simple yet profound answer. On a particularly rough night of verbal assault she closed her eyes and distinctly felt God's presence. It was as if He were saying out loud to her, "It is not about you, my daughter. This is about him and me." Slowly she learned to depend on God and it became a great joy to see the love of Jesus restore a wounded heart. Her husband wanted her to stay in the "I am worthless" mode, but God had other plans. The light that shines from her eyes speaks of the "care and feeding" of a gracious and great God. He became her husband—a faithful, trustworthy husband. The fidelity she sought in a human relationship and was so brutally denied was found in a dependable, sovereign God who loved her. "I think I kept my balance by using all of the Five Footholds, but survival started with total dependence on a God who saw me, knew me and loved me." The picture of Hagar's being comforted by God came clearly to mind. Charity, too, was a woman cast out and deserted. But God knew her name and promised her a "way in the wilderness—a new way."

Jesus loves me, this I know

"I grew up in a Christian environment without doubts of love, human or divine. But until I hit the wall I didn't know that He REAL-LY loved me!" How many of us can say "amen" to Alicia's statement? "When my confinement was over I missed the breath by breath dependence on the Lord. I wouldn't go back through that fire again, but it was a time of devotion and closeness that changed my life." Her words touched me deeply because I could absolutely identify. When life puts you on the mat it is awfully comforting to know that He is right there with us. Depending on Him takes everything we have—and that is just the point. It is all of Him and none of us. What a blessed paradox.

David Jeremiah tells the story of Karl Barth, the Swiss theologian. He came to the country in the 1960s to give a series of lectures. After one of his addresses, Barth was asked, "What is the greatest thought that has ever passed through your mind?" Barth paused for quite a while with his head down as he thought about his answer. The suspense mounted! What brilliant insight was this world famous theologian going to share? Finally, he raised his head and with childlike simplicity said, "Jesus loves me! This I know, for the Bible tells me so."

The bridge from our inadequacy to His sufficiency

The knowledge that Jesus loves me is the bridge from our inadequacy to His sufficiency. Do you know that Jesus loves you? I grew up in a loving home experiencing the broadest exposure to "all things Christian." If stopped on the street and questioned I would have quickly answered, "Oh, yes, Jesus loves me." But not until my forties did I have to dig in my heels and find His footing for my life. As my 20 year marriage ended and I struggled to rebuild my life the truth of the children's song sank into my soul. Yes, He did love me! Not because I was lovable, but because He was love.

The cross of Christ is the path between my inadequacy and God's sufficiency. The enemy wants us to linger and waste away in our inadequacy. God wants us to cross over to fullness in Him. In John Bunyan's Pilgrim's Progress young Christian on his way to the Celestial City falls into a bog called the Slough of Despond.

A man came to him whose name was HELP, and asked him what he did there?

"Sir," said CHRISTIAN, "I was bidden to go this way by a man called EVANGELIST, who directed me also to that gate, that I might escape the wrath to come; and as I was going there, I fell in here."

"But why did you not look for the steps?"

"Fear followed me so hard, that I fled the next way and fell in."

Then said he, "Give me thy hand." So he gave him his hand, and he drew him out; and set him upon some ground, and bade him go on his way.

Then I stepped to him that plucked him out, and said, "Sir, wherefore, since over this place is the way from the city of Destruction to yonder gate, is it that this plat is not mended, that poor travellers might go thither with more security?"

And he said unto me, "This miry slough is such a place as cannot be mended: it is the descent whither the scum and filth that attends conviction for sin doth continually run; and therefore it is called the Slough of Despond. For still, as the sinner is awakened about his lost condition, there arises in his soul many fears and doubts, and discouraging apprehensions, which all of them get together, and settle in this place: and this is the reason of the badness of this ground."

Facing our inadequacy is one of two spiritual realities. *Grasping His sufficiency* is the other. Between the two realities lies a dangerous no man's land filled with spiritual mines. The enemy wants to overwhelm us with our nothingness without reinforcing the hope of our neediness. Our Lord reaches across the Slough to extend the hand of Jesus' completed work at Calvary. Just as "Help" came to rescue Christian, Jesus comes to draw us from the clutches of our accusing enemy. David's words inspire us: "He lifted me out of the slimy pit, out of the mud and mire; he set my feet on a rock and gave me a firm place to stand." (Psalms 40:2 New International Version)

Focusing on Him, not ourselves

The shift from I can to I can't is necessary for true dependence. But the ultimate shift is from I can't to He can.

Major Ian Thomas, in his classic, *The Saving Life of Christ*, writes of moving from "ego-centric to deo-centric." For me, this is the point of recognizing that it is the holiness of God that contains us, the love of Jesus that sustains us and the work of the Spirit that maintains us. John the Baptist phrased it this way, "He must increase and I must decrease." Therefore, the first step in facing these seasons of limitation is to know with Ian Thomas that "it is your living faith in the adequacy of the One who is in you which releases His divine action through you." Without Him we can do nothing; Within Him there is nothing that we can't do.

I once won a prestigious award for being a Can-Do person. We give much credit to people who get it done. For years I prided myself on being the go-to, can-do woman. Gradually the Lord entrusted me with situations that strained my resources to the breaking point. Praise be to Him that He did. How awful it would be to go through life operating only at the level of human adequacy. As I learned how little I actually could do and how my seasons were from His hand, I began the journey of understanding His sufficiency. To say that I have mastered total dependence would be blasphemy. To say that I hunger for it would be somewhat closer to the truth. To say that I struggle each and every day against crying out, "Myfelf, I'll do it myfelf!" is absolutely genuine.

Put away "can do" living

In the rough draft process I shared this foothold with Lana, a dear Christian sister. She wrote back, "Foothold #1 is so precious and powerful! It's right where I am struggling in my life. I so want to depend on Him and let go of my "can do it all" way of life. It is futile, wears me out, and is such a waste of God's plan for me—I know that and yet feel trapped daily in the pattern. How do I get out??? I beg Him daily to get me out of this pattern and love him as he deserves and count on him to pull me through to the other side where I truly lean on Him and give him all the glory He so deserves. I know it's within my grasp—I know it in the early morning hours when I am alone with Him journaling and studying everything I can get my hands on to know Him—and yet as daylight comes into the windows and I begin my day—it's like the morning and the lessons I learned never happened—frequently—not always—but frequently. This chapter is the core of life—not just your book. And the gentleman who told you that this is the #1 principle is so correct."

When we come to the end of ourselves we must know that He is truth—that He is dependable and that He is all in all. To seek release is to be captured by the Almighty God. In comprehending His sufficiency, especially in times of confinement and limitation we cling to the divine nature of His sufficiency. "Can any situation arise, or any circumstances for which He is not adequate? Any pressure, promise, problem, responsibility or temptation for which the Lord Jesus Himself is not adequate? If He truly is God, there cannot be a single one," is the magnificent proclamation of trust from Major Ian Thomas.

REFLECTION

Getting A Foothold

Our inadequacy and God's sufficiency is the first step toward stability in confinement.

Dependence, not independence is the goal for the Christian.

The shift from I can to I can't to He can is risky if our focus is inward not upward.

His loving Hand is on us every step of the way; He is trustworthy and dependable.

Gaining Ground

You are in a season of confinement. Perhaps you are in a dead-end job, or are home-schooling. You may be caring for a terminally ill spouse. How do you keep your footing?

David said, "He keeps me stable on my high places." What are your high places and how do you keep your grip?

To what are you clinging and to what are you holding?

How do you avoid falling into the Slough of Despond?

Where is God's kiln for you?

REFLECTION

Following His Footsteps

Dear Father,_____

_____

_____

_____

_____

_____

_____

_____

_____

_____Amen

MUSINGS & AMUSINGS

"Meltdown"

Where did the sob begin? Almost uncontrollably the wail began and took over my entire body. It was 2:00 in the morning. Mom had tried to get out of bed and merely ended up wedged in the hospital rails. How would I release her? If I lower the rails then she is crushed; if I lean over and try to lift her I risk a back injury that would make me as incapacitated as she is…please, God, help me rescue her!

Then the next 90 minutes are out of a Stephen King novel. Mom, who has lost almost all mobility thrashes, kicks, talks incessantly and pleads to die when not threatening to kill me. This has to end, but what can I do? I am powerless; I am out of control; I am incompetent. What can I do to protect her? NOTHING. Is she past the time when I can keep her at home? Are they right—have I taken on something that is hurtful for everyone? Have I truly failed? The wracking sobs began.

Dad, even in his deafness, is aware of my trauma and wakes up. "I have never heard you cry so hard." "I can't protect Mom; I can't do anything to get you out of bed." I CANNOT, I CANNOT, I CANNOT! I glance at him and a single tear is rolling down his cheek. He understands and he weeps because he, too, is powerless. But his tear reminds me that when we are weak, then He is strong. When we are empty, then He is full. Praise Jesus that in the night-time of frustration, pain and sorrow…HE CAN!

MUSINGS & AMUSINGS

"Emotional Hematoma"

"The blood has pooled creating a hematoma. Don't put pressure on it, don't prick it and it will naturally be absorbed into the body." Those were the instructions to Mom as she was being discharged. But all she could see was a monstrous red mound on her tiny arm. "What happened?" "What caused it?" I think I must have learned cause and effect from this little woman who still searches for who to blame, desperately hoping that it isn't her.

This week Mom was hospitalized for a seizure and Dad had cancer surgery.

Those 13 words are the "what caused it" of my emotional hematoma. No one can see the bulbous gathering, but it is as real as was Mom's. "Don't bang it—don't prick it—or you will cause damage." The emotions of this week have pooled in my spirit and I need time to reach equilibrium and reabsorption. In Dr. Swenson's language, I have lived in the red zone for way too long. My emotional thermostat has overheated.

It is time for some coolant and time for some comfort. Hopefully, it will come through resting, not ingesting. Christ is the answer—not chocolate.

Oh, Father, keep me from being banged around. Keep me from rushing the process. Be my bandage, be my protection, be my Savior for I can do nothing but lean on you.

Five Footholds For Seasons of Limitation

- **DEPEND ON GOD**
- **ACKNOWLEDGE THE REALITY**
- **GRASP GOD'S GRACE**
- **WORK WITH A NET...WORK**
- **MAKE IT COUNT**

"Open my eyes that I may see wonderful things in your Word. I am but a pilgrim here on earth."
Psalm 119:18 (The Living Bible)

"Day by day and with each passing moment, Strength I find to meet my trials here."
Carolina Saudell Berg

3

ACKNOWLEDGE THE REALITY

We have an "I am that I am" God in an "It is what it is" situation!

Vic Owen was a physically active 35 year old man with a wife, a 6 year old daughter and a 5 year old son. He went to work and enjoyed "just everyday life." He taught Sunday School for 5 and 6 year old children. It would suddenly and irreversibly change. Awakened by an apparent nightmare he soon realized that life would never be the same. Vic had suffered a rare brainstem stroke in his sleep that would take away virtually all movement, all speech, all sight, all independence and all hope for a normal future. For the last 15 years Vic Owen has been severely limited. He lives in a nursing home, totally immobilized except for eye movement and the gift of one spared muscle in his hand. With this and the use of special computer equipment that converts electrical impulses in his brain into computer-recognized language he maintains contact with others. His condition has a name: Locked In Syndrome. That is the reality of Vic's life. He had a choice to make—deny and deteriorate or acknowledge and accommodate. He captured the reality and renamed his condition: "locked in but not left out." "In teaching Sunday School I learned that I could survive anything." He calls it what it is but then lives to see how far his physical imprisonment can be stretched. He lives with the hope of recovery through technological advances. More importantly, he understands that he is not in control of his life's outcome. "I am like the feather in Forrest Gump, totally controlled by conditions beyond my control." In acknowledging his confinement he works toward mental and emotional release. He has made choices to break down the walls. "I have stopped watching soap operas all day and gotten on the Internet. I am able to e-mail friends and family and FAX my doctor. This gives a paralyzed person a lot of options. I have e-mailed Bill Clinton, George Bush and most people in the news. This gives a guy who cannot move a lot more perceived power."

God is real

We live in a world of virtual reality. We can't touch it, but we accept it. I have friends who employ VAs—virtual assistants. They don't see them, nor even talk with them. Their work relationship is strictly electronic. That may be the new reality, but thankfully, it isn't the reality of divine confinement. A website dedicated to the eastern art of I Ching addresses seasons of limitation in this way: "Experiencing confinement and/or exhaustion are some of the worst of times. There are various intensities and durations of exhaustion and/or confinement, but each person is required to find an effective way of dealing with his or her own private hell. If you have come to this site for spiritual support we place a warning! Enduring Principles does not buy into ideas of angels of Gods we can pray to and receive help during rough times." (www. enduringprinciples.com)

One of the foundational truths of divine confinement is that He is with us…He is Emanuel, God with us. We do not have to face these times alone, nor do we have to create spiritual models that artificially "stave off collective fear" as enduring principles believes. We have a God who "walks with us and talks with us and tells us we are His own," in the poetic words of C. Austin Miles.

Definition and discipline

Acknowledging reality implies that we accurately define it and then effectively handle it. Joe Friday of Dragnet was immediately recognized by his dead-pan demand, "Just the facts, ma'am, just the facts." Although it is more than that, it certainly starts there. Reality has an electrical current; reality has a wind current and our job is to always keep current! Which way is the power flowing? Which way is the ship moving? When Mom died I wrote to friends that I couldn't get my sea legs. Strangely, that was accurate for where she was had temporarily altered my destination and reoriented my shoreline. My compass was pulling to an eternal true north, not an earthly one. Dad commented that we now had a heavenly magnet. To deny this pull and to deny the lack of balance would have been foolish, if not destructive. A reality check is moving away from what you want your world to be to getting a grip on what it is. It is looking at our environment with almost a clinical, objective eye and naming it. We commonly speak of "getting our arms" around problems. Those of us who are less conceptually oriented wonder about the usefulness of that phrase. But it does speak to getting the measure of the situation. All diagnosticians want to know at the outset the current condition of their subjects. They measure and record; test and assess. However, the human psyche is complex and not easily charted. In seasons of confinement we can slip into false readings. Assessing reality requires discipline. We too easily minimize, dramatize, supersize or spiritualize. The answer is to REALIZE.

True Reality is Accurate

Realization is wrapped around accurate perception. Seeing God's patterns for our lives sometimes means standing on "tippy-toe" and stretching. Other times it means putting blinders on and looking straight ahead. One of the stakes that we can drive into the ground to hold our perceptions against the winds of confinement is the goodness of God. Another is that these seasons are "common to man (and woman)" and we aren't being singled out for some spooky journey. We sometimes find it hard to keep our times correctly measured. We don't want to blow it out of proportion by blaming God nor by assuming great personal guilt. I laughingly say that when they were passing out guilt, I thought they said "quilt" and I asked for king size! But I want to live in the light of truth and that means that I put away the guilt quilt and pull out the "loin girder" of Ephesians 6.

The Blessing of Reality

"Brenda, this is a difficult season for my wife. She does such a great job with the kids, but it isn't easy for her." This 6'4" man carries himself with confidence and great poise. Lee's day is filled making good things happen for the Kingdom of God. This is an exciting time in life for him. I was deeply touched by his loving sensitivity to his wife, Anne. She is a marriage partner whose current time revolves around creating a safe haven for Lee and their children. Together they decided that she would stay home with four children under age five. "Anne has four children?" Most people are shocked that this career-oriented woman not only has children but that she has devoted her life to them. She doesn't feel that she "has" to be there, she "gets" to be there. Reality to her is being God's blessing to her husband and children with all of her heart, mind and soul. In this season of limitation she is not half-hearted because she knows that God has called her to this time. But she doesn't super spiritualize it, either. She admits when the road is rocky and when she longs for a break. In our home we grew up with the poem that urges us to keep going "when nothing but the will says, 'go.'" Anne's family lives with a woman of will, but also of great heart.

Rationalization is counterproductive

Gloria is a 30ish woman with a promising career. From the outside she "has the whole package." But internally she is living through the difficulties of being single in a marriage-oriented culture; being stuck in a job that has played itself out; and being left with the repercussions of bad judgment in her 20s. As she talked about her feelings of limitation she brought home the importance of realizing, not rationalizing, where we are. "When I am boxed in I need to face up to it and accept it. It is so easy to want it to be something that it isn't." How tempting it is to take the "Calgon, take me away!" view of life. We dramatize the situation and look for a magical way of escaping where we are. But the bubbles eventually fade in the Calgon bath, the water grows cold and we need to put our pruney fingers to work.

You earlier met my friend Chris Miller. The lessons that she teaches "from the clay" inspire and motivate me. She is skillful and passionate about her work but in the spring of 2004 she had to face the harsh reality of limitation. " I went through a degenerative disc/sciatica thing that sent me to the ER, then to a chiropractor, now to a physical therapist—because in the process, I lost feeling in the left side of my foot and up the back of my left leg. Each step of the way, I have been encouraged to give up pottery. But I feel I have been called to be a potter. So each step of the way, my husband has helped me make adjustments with my wheel, etc., so that I can continue. But God is great. He has allowed this to happen to me, and has worked great things through it. It has given me a different perspective. I praise Him for this time." She didn't minimize the circumstances, nor did she ignore the consequences. Freedom came when she accepted the "what is" and the "Who is."

The Attitude of Victory

The world tells us that we can master our circumstances by a mind over matter attitude. But these are tough matters for tough minds. It isn't called a trial for nothing. We weren't told to consider it all fun, but to consider the deep, abiding joy that comes through His hand. Often we run away emotionally before our feet ever leave the ground.

How easy it would be to dramatize Vic's situation—for it is a tragedy. But he wastes no time whining. Nurse practitioner Brenda Ziegler says that Vic "continues to be an inspiration to us all. He is caring and compassionate as he helps others in similar situations." When his feet were sliding he chose a winner's attitude. The story is told of Alexander the Great's being presented with a young soldier accused of cowardice. "What is your name?" the Commander asked. "Alexander," he answered almost inaudibly. "I can't hear you, what is your name?" "Alexander," he loudly answered. "Son, either change your name or change your attitude." No one will ever have to give Victor Owen that choice for he triumphantly lives up to his name!

God's Reminders of His plan

Elisabeth Elliot, cherished Christian writer and speaker, addresses the response of the believer in seasons of confinement. As a young widow she certainly saw God's working and contemplated what her reaction should be. She exemplifies how we acknowledge the reality when she says: "We cannot always or even often control events, but we can control how we respond to them. When things happen which dismay or appall, we ought to look to God for His meaning, remembering that He is not taken by surprise nor can His purposes be thwarted in the end. What God looks for is those who will worship Him in the midst of every circumstance. Our look of inquiring trust glorifies Him. This is our first responsibility: to glorify God. In the face of life's worst reversals and tragedies, the response of a faithful Christian is praise—not for wrong itself, certainly, but for who God is and for the ultimate assurance that there is a pattern being worked out for those who love Him."

The 38th chapter of Exodus outlines details of the tabernacle. Verse 8 says: "The bronze washbasin and its bronze pedestal were cast from the solid bronze mirrors donated by the women who assembled at the entrance to the Tabernacle." (The Living Bible) Each time that Aaron and his sons went in to appear before the Lord or burn offerings they were required to wash their hands and feet. As they washed they caught sight of their own faces in the bowls and remembered that these sacrifices were for them, as well as the other people of God. This was a holy acknowledgement of reality. We, too, must see our face in God's laver. As we offer ourselves in seasons of limitation we know that He has designed this altar for us.

God's Sustaining Presence

"I am just not made to sit in an office pushing papers! But lots of people do what they don't want to do." John's season of limitation was created by a micro-managing boss whose management style was "surprise the people and catch them napping." But John was the director of development and his job was to fund a sizeable annual budget. This wasn't done sitting in an office; he had to be with the donors. He had come to me for Myers-Briggs Type Indicator (MBTI) coaching. Clearly God had not designed him for life in a windowless office with cups of over-sharpened pencils and very stale coffee. What was the first step? Acknowledge the reality. He knew Whose he was, but he was losing who he was in this season. He initially ignored the warning signs of restlessness, frustration and lack of productivity. He was minimizing the reality. He agreed that he was not in this situation by accident. He was in God's gymnasium, as Dad always says. He was seeing God use this time to affirm his gifts and certainly his "non-gifts." Pushing for a fit denied him the power to learn what he could and then head for the exit door. *Seeing the truth allowed him to know that we have an "I am that I am" God in an "It is what is it" situation.*

Dawn Rochelle sat pensively across the table from me as we talked about our divine confinements. I was under house arrest with the full-time care of two elderly and fragile parents; she was caring for a disabled sibling with no imminent release. This season is looking long and hard. She lifted her eyes and said that she understood the necessity for acknowledging the reality. She told me of her caregiving and then poignantly remarked, "He is heavy, but he's my brother." There was no effort to shift the weight—it was hers, given to her by God. Victor Hugo, the French philosopher, puts it in perspective: "Have courage for the great sorrow of life and patience for the small ones. And when you have laboriously accomplished your daily task, go to sleep in peace. God is awake." He never slumbers, nor does He sleep. When he gives us a task to accomplish He gives us the strength and watches over us unceasingly. "How precious it is, Lord, to realize that you are thinking about me constantly! I can't even count how many times a day your thoughts turn towards me. And when I wake in the morning, you are still thinking of me!" (Psalm 139: 17,18–The Living Bible) Dawn Rochelle knows this God whose eye sees her.

Susan's bright smile greets her patients belying her serious physical deterioration. Lupus is robbing her of balance, strength and agility. The sixty hour weeks she happily devoted to gerontology have now been reduced to part time work. She knows that she won't regain her lost capabilities; she knows that further deterioration is inevitable. "How do you live with that?" I asked. "I don't look back. I enjoy who I was but I appreciate who I am." She not only acknowledges reality, but models it with a glad heart. As we were talking she mentioned a prayer request. Assuming that it related to her limitation I was surprised to hear her ask for intercession on behalf of her 100 year old father. Focusing on others keeps our perspective clear. Sensing God's presence keeps our feet on the path.

Dialysis University

My Dad has been blessed with a very long, accomplished life. Long ago he committed his life to "stretching others." His impact as a business executive, writer, speaker and mentor extraordinaire has changed the lives of thousands. His physical strength has always amazed our family. Although a childhood injury resulted in his having the use of only one hand he has managed great feats of endurance. Complemented by his mental, spiritual and emotional disciplines, he has been a man of great productive strength. In 1999 my Dad underwent a 180 degree life turn. His kidneys failed due to prolonged hypertension. Three times a week he undergoes dialysis. There is no recovery. This season of limitation will last until he is called to heaven, joining Mom. To process this change and create a set of operating principles he wrote a piece affectionately known as *Dialysis University*. To me, it is the definitive expression of acknowledging reality. With his permission it is being reprinted in its entirety for your benefit.

Dialysis University

My life has permanently changed. I accept the change; now I must try to understand it. In order to get the most from the change I must consider myself, at 84, to have enrolled in a new school which I call DU (Dialysis University) with classes three days a week for four hours each.

There are certain unique features to DU. The teachers share the responsibility with me. They keep me alive with their medical skill and I decide what courses of learning to follow from a great variety of possibilities, the first being a comprehensive understanding of the full dialysis process. They provide the quality time and I decide what I will do with the time. It is a joint responsibility.

Another unique feature of DU is the lack of a graduation; therefore, a diploma doesn't determine the course selection. Exit from the school is entrance into eternity.

In order to maximize the experience I have decided to adopt a philosophy of dialysis that will guide me as I progress. I have put it into writing so that I might read and review until it becomes a mental/spiritual habit and eventually a living reflex.

Constructive Adjustments To Dialysis:

1. Gratitude for the discipline rather than rebellion against the restrictions. I am being helped rather than restricted. This discipline assures life.

2. Respect the diet: It is not what I can't have, it's that I don't want what I should not have. Abstinence is positive, not negative.

3. The expenses: I'm making an investment in a quality of life, not being forced to spend money on assistance that I once didn't require.

4. Recognize the variable value of time: Spend the most valuable hours on the most valuable activities. Have interesting, productive things to do during the hours of energy. Don't fret about the survival mode in down times. I am only responsible for what I can do, not for what I would like to do or think that I should do. Only my capability is my responsibility.

5. Guard against negative thoughts and remarks, either within myself or with others. I am not competing in a health race with

others. Accept that sickness can be destructive to a proper attitude. Disciplined silence can be constructive.

6. I consider my sickness as normal, therefore in no part divine punishment. Nothing is happening to me "that is not common to man."

7. Be careful not to lose the good of this difficult situation. Look for each bit of good and express appreciation for it. I believe that God is in my circumstances mysteriously, even though I can't understand or definitely define each element. Faith, therefore, is a major factor in my adjustment.

8. The situation is for life: Therefore I must take the long view and not be occupied or anxious about every up and down blip on the screen. Up times will be limited just the same as the down times. It is good to remember, "This, too, shall pass."

9. Dialysis may alter my way of life but will not define it. I am not living to have dialysis; I am having dialysis in order to live. Therefore it will not dominate my thoughts nor conversation. It is a means to provide quality life.

10. I will not use my dialysis to control my family or friends.

11. In early dialysis I've had some experiences of the joy of life that helped me to understand Paul's acceptance of his "thorn" or Solzhenitsyn's gratitude for "the stinking straw." Suffering's chief function is to purify...purify our thinking and promote the growth of our faith.

Hail to Old DU!
My choice: Be a victim or a victor.
Copyright © Fred Smith, Sr. 1999

You may never be on dialysis. But you may have experienced one of those 180 degree turns. My life's turn came as Mom and Dad moved into my house. I tried to minimize, supersize, dramatize and spiritualize but the answer came when I realized that God is here. He wants us to know that the way to handle our seasons of confinement is to acknowledge the reality of Who He is and Whose we are. He truly shows us that we have an "I am God in an it is what it is situation."

REFLECTION

Getting A Foothold

1. Stability comes through seeing and acknowledging the truth.
2. Realize—don't minimize supersize, dramatize or spiritualize
3. Our seasons are from God's hand; our feet rest upon Him.
4. His eyes never close; He is always awake.

Gaining Ground

1. What is my current reality?
2. How am I running away?
3. Who helps me guard my heart and mind?
4. Do I minimize, dramatize, supersize or spiritualize?
5. Is my compass properly calibrated?

REFLECTION

Following His Footsteps

Dear Father,_____

_____

_____

_____

_____

_____

_____

_____

_____Amen

MUSINGS & AMUSINGS

"Rock and Roll Woman"

"Excuse me, I don't mean to intrude, but could I ask about your basket?" The woman behind me in the checkout line was noticing a basket full of Depends, Pampers, Baby Wipes and Incontinence Bed Pads. Without thinking, I looked at her and responded, "I am a rock and roll woman—I'm rocking my grandchildren and rolling my parents." After I said it I realized that it was an identity cry like that of my earlier years, "I am woman." We are **not** the sandwich generation. Who wants to be the salami between two slices of stale rye? No, we are the women of the 60's who are now rocking and rolling. But just like the wheels came off our supermom, you-can-have-it-all bicycles, we are struggling to keep this phase in balance. Where does the line get drawn on what needs to be done and what is nice to be done? Where does responsibility take the place of spontaneous responsiveness? At the same time I mentally bowed my head and thanked the Lord that I was privileged to have both jobs. In my twenties I could rock and roll all night; at 60 it is a lot harder. Poodle skirts and bobby sox have long since disappeared but the rock and roll woman is still very much alive.

MUSINGS & AMUSINGS

"Are You Scared?"

"Grandmother, are you scared?" His 4 year old face was pressed against her 87 year old countenance. She had been taken to the emergency room after passing out. I thought she had died in my arms in a most immodest and ignoble heap on the floor. She revived only to be put through a physician's multiple-page testing regimen. What value could there be in subjecting her to endless probes and proddings? As Andrew asked the question I knew that he was asking his own question. Each of us standing around the bed is scared, but masking it through silence, extraversion or aggravated anguish. It took his innocent question to break through. We weren't avoiding the consideration of death—we were firmly convinced that her eternal life was to be immeasurably better than this dying process. But we wanted it to be with grace and decorum, not with wires and the anonymity of institutional care. "Are you scared?" What a wonderful question. Every caregiver needs to give truthful consideration and answer from a "soul place." Scared of failing in the task, scared of imbalanced sibling relationships, scared of crucial career decisions, scared of responsibility, scared of seeing no way out…Jesus knows that we are scared and offers refuge. He shows us that in Him caregiving moves from a place of being *scared* to a place of being *sacred*.

MUSINGS & AMUSINGS

"Wheeling and Dealing"

She smiled at me on the elevator. The poignant irony of the situation was impossible to ignore. As I worked to readjust the wheelchair she mirrored my efforts. As we quietly waited for the floors to pass we looked at each other and recognized that we were on two ends of life's spectrum. Her toddler and my Mom were locked in animated conversation; she and I were tacitly expressing the fact that each of us had a treasured child: one in a stroller and one in a wheelchair. The doors opened, we separated but shared a special moment of understanding that we each had precious cargo and a God-given responsibility. One was expectantly looking forward to leaving the stroller behind while I was anxiously wanting to hold onto these days of wheelchair Malling. She would see him grow up and leave home; I would watch Mom grow old and go home.

Five Footholds For Seasons of Limitation

- **DEPEND ON GOD**
- **ACKNOWLEDGE THE REALITY**
- **GRASP GOD'S GRACE**
- **WORK WITH A NET...WORK**
- **MAKE IT COUNT**

"My grace is sufficient for you."
2 Corinthians 12:9 (New International Version)

"Marvelous, infinite, matchless grace,
Freely bestowed on all who believe!"
Julia H. Johnson

4

GRASP GOD'S GRACE

With His grace we can handle all that He hands us

My Mom's entire life was dedicated to her family. Her face would light up just seeing us across a room. Spending time with the family's four generations would always evoke, "Now this is living!" She cooked, cleaned and shopped with total abandon. Hers was a life of service. She conquered a life-threatening brain tumor and rebounded to laugh about her stylishly short hair. No one met her who wasn't encouraged with a kind word, a listening ear and a quick smile. A drooping expression led my physician uncle to diagnose her as with Parkinson's disease, a degenerative condition. My very first thought was of the inevitable limitations. Her movement, her agility, her quick wit and her eager hug would all be locked uselessly away into a body that no longer responded to brain cues. We were all forced to admit where we were and commit the situation to God. Mom's strength carried all of us until her frail body could no longer support her and we gladly accepted the responsibility of carrying her.

As her Parkinson's worsened her nighttime restlessness increased. A period of night terrors would shake her body. When asleep she would call out for me during periods of immobility, bad dreams or general fear. Instead of Brenda, she would call me Grace, the name of her older sister. For the years that we lived together I heard her call out "Grace! Grace!' night after night. Before I could get a running start down the hall she would be repeating it over and over. Even in her half-asleep state she wanted help. In my half-asleep state I wanted to roll over and ignore the call. For years it was my Dad's job to be the first responder—he was her bedmate. But clearly as he grew less able the responsibility became mine. Finally his graduation to a hospital bed meant that this was now totally "my job." I bought Fisher-Price baby monitors that turned my entire house into one large nursery suite. "Grace, Grace" reverberated throughout. Months became years and the more sleep deprived I became the less I was able to perform at my self-imposed level of competence. One night God stepped into my consciousness and hit me over the head. Every time Mom called out—sometimes every 30 minutes—I was being reminded that this job wasn't possible through my own strength, but only through His grace. *Sounds in the night were no longer the problem but reminders of the solution. What He hands me I can handle through His grace.*

What is that in your hand?

Steve Brown of Key Life Ministries is dedicated to "getting you and those you love, Home with freedom, joy and faithfulness to Christ as your crowning achievement." While speaking at The Billy Graham Training Center at The Cove, Steve unpacked the short story related in Exodus 4:2-4. "What do you have in your hand?" The Lord asked him. And he replied, "A shepherd's rod." "Throw it down on the ground, "the Lord told him. So he threw it down—and it became a serpent, and Moses ran from it! Then the Lord told him, "Grab it by the tail! He did, and it became a rod in his hand again! As only Steve Brown can, he drew out this story to help us see where we were forfeiting the freedom that God has provided in Jesus. "What is your rod?" was his question to us. "What is He asking you to throw down so that He can reconfigure it for His glory?"

Moses had depended on that shepherd's staff for protection, support and as a symbol of his livelihood during those years of exile. He undoubtedly had dealt with many snakes in the protection of his father-in-law's flock. As Steve says, "I bet Moses was pretty attached to that staff. And I know for sure that he was smart enough not to pick up a snake from the tail end!" But God was answering the plea of Moses for validation. "I have no clout, Lord! You have given me a job with all responsibility and no authority—no fair."

Later on that evening I sat in my room alone meditating on Steve's question: "What is in your hand?" I had come away for that weekend to rest from a period of intense caregiving. I had come to be renewed and refreshed in a wearisome task. "What is in your hand, Brenda?" With great humbleness the answer came: the martyrdom of caregiving. But how could they know I was doing the work of God if I didn't moan and groan like Jeremiah? Then the clarity of conviction came. I wasn't called to be Jeremiah; I was called to be Fred and Mary Alice's daughter Brenda and I was to throw down the shepherd's staff and pick up the Rod of God! I was to lay down martyrdom and pick up faithful service. He would be the support, the protection and the symbol of the work that He had given me to do. What is in your hand today? Throw it down right now.

Falling Short

Initially I called this Foothold "Practice Forgiveness." I thought that one way we lose our footing in these seasons is to fall into the perfectionism trap. So, the logical way out is to admit that we are only human and move on. That recognition isn't nearly enough...it is that I am a sinner gripped by the grace of God to perform His work as only He can do it. Otherwise, we set unattainable goals and create unworkable expectations only to fail. The world says that falling doesn't matter as long as we get up. Quite to the contrary, the falling is important as it is our means to His lifting us up.

Webster says that perfectionism is "disposition which regards anything short of perfect as unacceptable." In historic Christendom a group of theologians called Palegians established a doctrine of perfectibility. It is the hackneyed "every day in every way I am getting better and better. Social Darwinism at its best. All they would have to do is live with me for 24 hours to see the fundamental flaw in their thinking.

The dictionary phrase, "anything short" is reminiscent of Paul's statement in Romans. "All have sinned and fall short of the glory of God." We miss the mark. Remember the illustration of the archers all lined up and shooting for the target only to have their arrows descend before striking? That is a familiar word picture for sin. We are unable to hit the target. Only God can achieve the desired result that doesn't fall short. So, a perfectionistic attitude isn't just a hindrance in seasons of limitation—it is sin. It is assuming that we are capable of something that only God Himself can attain. The "I will be as the Most High" attitude resulted in an angel of light's hasty and eternal departure from heaven. The prophet Amos boldly stated, "You alone are God." There is relief in recognizing that efforts to be perfect are going to be leaky water pitchers. Grace is about hope. Grace is about seeing that there is only one job opening for God—and it is filled!

God's Good

Carolyn Thomas knows what it means to literally face confinement. In 2003 a jealous boyfriend fired a gun at her point blank and virtually blew her face away. Rather than choose bitterness and revenge she committed herself to finding the meaning, however obscured it may be. "I'm alive for a reason. I don't question God." God is doing through us in these difficult times. He wants us to see the good in a bad situation. More importantly, He wants us to see His good in our bad situations. He wants us to accept these times as a gift from a good God…a grace gift. He is interested in doing through me. It is His life in me that will come through these confinements. Are you in a bad relationship? Does your job feel like a dead-end? Are you overwhelmed by the demands of raising three children under age four? God wants to work through you. He wants to shower the grace and to receive the glory.

Under stressful conditions it is not uncommon to feel out of control. Our hands are tied behind our backs and we will exercise whatever power we think we have. We strive thinking that we will thrive. But this is a counterfeit attitude and a substitute for His holy substitution. Perfectionism isn't an expression of who we are in Christ for He is the perfect one, not us. What we want to see is who He is in us. It is ALL ABOUT HIM! Anything else is all about us. The clever ploy of the enemy is that it all looks so good. It looks like we are striving for holiness, seeking for righteousness and pursuing Godliness. And indeed, it is all of those things, but it is OUR striving, OUR seeking, OUR pursuing. To stay standing in life's prisons requires falling at His feet.

Perfectionistic Temperature

Dr. Bill Gaultiere, Executive Director of New Hope Crisis Counseling at the Crystal Cathedral has constructed an informal inventory to take your "perfectionistic temperature." Check out any of these statements that apply to you. No one will be watching, so be real.

"I often think I should have done better than I did."
"I tend to put things off if I can't do them perfectly."
"I'm afraid to fail when I'm doing an important project."
"I think less of myself if I repeat the same mistake."
"I strive to maintain control of my emotions at all times."
"I get upset when things don't go as planned."

"I am often disappointed in the quality of other people's lives."
"I am afraid that people will think less of me if I fail."
"I'm unhappy if anything I do is considered average."
"I'm constantly trying to improve myself."
"I feel inferior to others who are more intelligent, attractive or successful than I."

When I honestly responded I felt God's arrows ventilating my entire spirit. Who was this about? It was about me. Who does He want it to be about? HIM! Perfection is not only an impossibility, but a totally inappropriate goal.

An online Apology Room features line after line of text from people who want to enter this cyberconfessional.

"To My Dad: I am sorry that on this night that you have gone to be with God I have let you down so much."

"To My Sons: I'm sorry I'm not the kind of Mom you deserve, the kind of Mom I long to be."

Guilt and Grace

Can you hear the admission of failure? They have taken step one: they have recognized their inadequacy. Unless they accept the gift of Jesus' work they won't move on to total dependence. Certainly they have taken the step of acknowledging their reality, painful as it may be. It could be that they are on a spiritual journey that has brought them to the edge of the Slough. Human perfectionism will always bring us to the end. We then see the tension between where we are and where we could be. Dad makes a clear distinction that the difference between where we are and where we should be generates guilt; the difference between where we are and where we could be generates excitement.

Guilt requires a lifetime of payments; grace pays a lifetime of dividends. "Grace, as Dr. Gerald D. May observes in his thoughtful book *Addiction and Grace*, "seeks us but will not control us." A powerful story is told of Beverly Sills, the magnificent operatic soprano. She was hosting a small party in her apartment overlooking the grand city of New York. One of the guests came up to her and asked if she shouldn't be leaving soon. "Why?" "I thought you had to sing tonight at the Met." "No, I don't have to sing tonight." A short exchange followed between the guest and Ms. Sills. "I saw you listed on the program." After a dramatic pause, she remarked, "I don't have to sing—I get to sing." Guilt says, "I have to;" grace says, "I get to."

Cease The Striving

When we are in situations that confine us, limit us, and restrain us we often think initially it will bring out the best in us. We muster our strength, martial our resources and develop a game plan. Without the fundamentals of faith we will end up striving instead of abiding. We will forget that He can do when we cannot. He is in the doing through us business. It is the "marvelous grace of our loving Lord, grace that exceeds our sin and our guilt" that moves us through the darkness. Newton captured the essence of grace as he wrote, "The Lord has promised good to me, His word my hope secures; He will my shield and portion be as long as life endures."

Briana is a beautiful woman in her early fifties. When we first met she was on the "must know" list in my world of women's marketing. Her poise, confidence and authenticity immediately drew me to her. We quickly found that our shared faith gave us more than "women in the marketplace" issues to discuss. Moving through the levels of communication was done easily. Soon we were talking deeply, sharing what God had done in lives composed of the brightest, most sparkling threads as well as dark, heavy fibers. Her life story was one of dichotomies; her journey was one of contradictions. The ambivalence was understood when she said, "I am a sinner, saved by grace.

I think about all the years I spent being what I thought I was supposed to be—never really identifying what made me tick. I was afraid to. What if what I am is not enough—not successful enough—not smart enough—not anything enough! I've lived with that for so long—it is a breath of fresh air to be living the real me that God created." When we are confined we have a choice: gasp or grasp.

Rodney is a successful attorney who has recently been diagnosed with malignant melanoma. He called to catch up and described the series of chemotherapy and radiation treatments that he is undergoing after cancer surgery. "God is so good. He is faithfully seeing me through all of this. Of course, I am in the best physical shape of my life. My wife has me on a strict nutritional regimen and I am really taking care of myself. I decided to take control of this treatment program and I am going to get through with flying colors because I am on top of the situation." He was faced with a box and he was going to be the best that there had ever been in the oncology department's history. He was going for the gold star!

Briana and Rodney have one thing in common: they want to do their best. What is wrong with that? Doesn't the Bible say, "Be ye perfect, even as I am perfect?" Yes, but I think a more suitable translation is Be mature—GROW UP! "We will in all things grow up into Him who is the Head, that is, Christ." (Ephesians 4:14–New International Version). An alternative approach is to strive for excellence, not perfection. But Ian Thomas dispels this aspiration in his discussion of Moses: "God would have us know without any shadow of ambiguity that no degree of human excellence can ever be a substitute for His dear Son. Moses did his best. His very, very best—but this was the mistake that Moses made! For God was waiting to do God's best to give only what can be given, from the risen, living Rock!"

Response To His Faithfulness

The book of James introduces us to the balance between faith and works. We are saved through grace by faith; we are to continue in good works. Seasons of confinement are by His hand—His loving hand—His hand of grace. Our response is to be one of faithful discipline. The three stewards who were entrusted with coins were expected to multiply their value. So we are to demonstrate in our confinements the increased grace of God.

"Prepare your minds for action; be self-controlled." (I Peter 1:13–New International Version)

Amanda is an international consultant with homes in South America and the United States. As an early teenager living in Europe she was told that any further education would be her total responsibility. With limited financial resources she applied to an American university to pursue an education degree, ultimately receiving her doctorate. When others spent weekends with friends, she stayed in the dorm to study. While her classmates traveled and socialized she worked on campus and kept to herself, learning a new language and managing on meager funds. How did she survive? Mental and emotional discipline. She told me her story in a very matter of fact manner still knowing that what she had accomplished was quite beyond the ordinary. "I was lonely, but I knew that I had a purpose and nothing would deter me. I was convinced that God had a better plan for me and would open the doors. It was hard but I trusted and kept on working." She had faith, but she faithfully executed a plan of action.

Mental Discipline

Foothold #2 features Dad's writing on Dialysis University. I hope that you have taken time to really study his points—it is like mining for diamonds. Since that time he has become immobilized, unable to move by himself. To undergo dialysis he must be transported on gurney-like equipment known as the Barton Chair. For us it is a miraculous invention. Day after day he either lies hooked to a dialysis machine or in his hospital bed unable to move except with the help of family or home health care workers. How easy it would be to become discouraged, depressed or even in despair. At night he experiences hours of restlessness and inability to sleep. Many would be challenged to see the quality in this life. But he teaches me and all others around him that in true seasons of limitation mental and emotional discipline is the doorway to appropriating God's grace. He believes that this confinement is superintended by the hand of a loving God. But he also understands that he has the responsibility of a correct response. Frankl's work, Man's Search For Meaning, was mealtime fare at our house as we grew up. Some families read the comics to each other; Dad read Oswald Chambers, Brother Lawrence and Victor Frankl's classic, *Man's Search for Meaning*. While imprisoned during World War II this brilliant psychotherapist concluded that we often have no control over our circumstances, but we have the ultimate freedom of choosing our attitude. I now see that for Dad this was not idle intellectualism; it was preparation for an extended season of confinement that would be publicly witnessed just as the imprisonment of others before him. "Are you comfortable?" "Comfort really isn't the question—'is it tolerable?' would be better." This answer is from a man who has traveled hundreds of thousands of miles speaking and consulting but is now confined by hospital bed rails.

Self-Control

"Read Proverbs 16:32" was the cryptic note from Dad. I was in the midst of a devastating personal experience and I wasn't handling it particularly well. "Better a patient man than a warrior, a man who controls his temper than one who takes a city." Self-control, Brenda, self-control. That was nearly 20 years ago and I am still a learner. Watching beloved parents grow frail and move toward heaven is an emotionally draining task. Doing it in front of home health care workers, friends and family is almost unbearable at times. The loss of privacy, the struggle to carve out an invisible place in which to exist wears out even the heartiest. On one such night I prayed out loud, "Father, you know every breath and every minute of this time. You can create in me a clean spirit and give me self-control. You can cause love to grow where only irritation now exists. You can shine through the hardness of my heart to display your mercy and grace." Dad's twenty year old message rang through to me...you don't have to take a city, just take control. Didn't He tell me that His grace was sufficient?

Self-control is a discipline that is directly related to spiritual growth. It is part of that spiritual fruit bowl that is always appropriate "in and out of season." Walking in the Spirit is far preferable to pacing the perimeter of my prison and decrying the inequities of life. When our feet are slipping it is helpful to have built in fail-safe systems established. The discipline of regular Bible study and prayer opens the way to a Spirit-led perspective on our confinement. Oftentimes the words of David will break the fall and bring us into the presence of God. We may land with a thud, but we are before Him.

Humor in the Box

Humor is an outlet for stress. Confinement gets serious and taking it too seriously can warp our perspective. But it isn't always easy to find the laugh. Did you ever think about how hard it is to laugh when you are tied in knots? Melanie was in a management meeting hearing news that her 21 year job was in jeopardy. She could feel the prison walls closing in on her. For the last three years she had been feeling the physical and emotional effects of career uncertainty. Now the day had finally arrived. As the CEO stood before their team and described the new organizational chart she suddenly realized that the room needed some fresh air. Almost spontaneously she made a funny remark that broke the tension and eased the meeting. Life isn't funny for Melanie, but she understands that life is too serious not to laugh. Refusing to laugh robs us of healthy balance. Developing our humorous reflexes enhances the value of our confinements. Humor puts gripper soles on our shoes and keeps us in the game.

Seasons of limitation often get very uni-dimensional. All we see is our side of the cell wall. But there are always two sides to every environment, situation and issue. One life lesson that I try to remember is "even the flattest pancake has two sides!" When we remove humor from our prison we have taken away the release valve. Too often we focus on ourselves and our situation to the exclusion of any levity. The theater understands that the deepest tragedy engenders the most uproarious laughter. They call it the human condition. In these times it is not just helpful, but absolutely necessary, to find smiles in each day. Sometimes these smiles will burst into laughter and surprise everyone. Tom lost the "love of his life." It seemed easy for people to gather around him and share his grief. It was much more difficult to bring a smile. Laughter in the midst of sorrow seemed disrespectful, even sacrilegious. I felt that my job was to nudge him toward finding smiles during the day so I challenged him to find one good laugh…and to keep count. "I had eight last week" was his greeting to me as we passed at church. He was not disregarding the mourning, but finding that "joy comes in the morning."

Emotional Discipline

Cindy and I were talking about emotional discipline when she commented, "Many of our decisions on how we react or respond are based on what we think people will think of us, or what we will look like to others if we do or don't do a certain thing. That's an "inside-out" perspective, where we begin with US, our feelings inside, and then base our actions on what we believe will be most appropriate based on what others will say, or what "normal" people do. When we do this, we get very attached and protective of US. A self-centeredness that is very unhealthy occurs. We can stop and take an Outside-In perspective. It frees me from basing my thoughts and actions on what I believe others believe about me. I can just DO IT." Seasons of confinement offer danger and opportunity: the danger of asking, "How do I look" and the opportunity of "looking to see how." Too often we think of our confinements as mirrored boxes. All we see is our own reflection. In divine confinement we learn how to look to Him and not at ourselves. Focusing externally broadens our emotional base and lengthens our stride.

Michelle is twenty. We were the only two in the exercise room so I thought I would ask for her feedback, fully expecting a blank stare. "When I say limitation and confinement what comes to mind? For the next 30 minutes she told a story of family dysfunction, life choices and moving 1500 miles away from everyone that she knew. Her story of emotional, financial and even physical risk taking left me breathless. At twenty she knew more about imprisonment than most 40 year olds. "How did you work through this?" "I figured out what I needed to do to be healthy and started taking steps to make it happen."

She wasn't hindered by what she didn't have, but focused on what she needed to keep moving. A stillness of heart and clarity of mind center us to take constructive action.

Physical Care

"R and R" became a slang term for military leave. It was time for rest and relaxation. Long periods of intense stress and battle action depleted the mental and physical states of servicemen. Fatigue and depression are the natural outcome of prolonged seasons of confinement. In life coaching we talk about "self-care." As a Christian often I chafe at the term. But running out of gas through "selflessness" is actually more selfish. Are you working 70 hours a week and proud of it? Are you wearing burn-out as a badge of honor? Have you taken a break from the responsibilities of home schooling or are you indispensable? Are you finding the difficult balance between care provision and 24/7 duty?

Elijah found himself in a season of emotional confinement while running from Jezebel. He ran until he was exhausted and then sat down praying to die. "I have had enough, Lord," he said. "Take my life." "All at once an angel touched him and said, 'Get up and eat.' ...The angel of the Lord came back a second time and touched him and said, 'Get up and eat for the journey is too much for you...Strengthened by that food, he traveled."

For me, the shift from martyrdom to faithful service in caregiving means accepting the responsibility of self-care. Understanding my dietary and sleep requirements is not just theoretical. It is important to eat right, to fight for proper sleep and to make time for spiritual refreshment. The Lord brought bread of life and living water to Elijah and he does that for us, as well. "Are you eating enough and are you getting exercise?" If you are in confinement you have probably heard that from family and friends. The concern is well-focused. Physical discipline during these seasons can impact the quality of both the confinement and the life following. Taking time for you in order to better serve requires strict discipline. Taking time for you in order to faithfully endure requires God's grace.

The Discipline of Gratitude

Grace is an unearned, undeserved gift. Seasons of confinement seem unearned and undeserved, as well. The nature of the gift is often harder to recognize. "It isn't fair" quickly comes to our minds. As we think we are holding to Him we learn that we are actually "in His grip." To regain footing means knowing that house arrest is indeed a gift from the hand of a loving God. "In all things give thanks for this is the will of God concerning you." Perhaps the discipline of gratitude is the most demanding. Dad always reminds me that it is difficult to be thankful and grouchy simultaneously...they create mutually exclusive mental activity. God's power is released in our weakness and the access code is encrypted into our thankfulness.

MaryLou's prayer journal reflects a time of intense pain and confinement. For years she has lived with a drug-addicted husband, fearful for herself and her children. She has been lost in the mire of the "what-ifs" losing sight of God's graciousness. Self- analysis and self-pity have created a toxic environment that stifled spiritual growth. The decontamination process began as she could express her thanks to God. "How could I ever begin to understand the way to give thanks? Perhaps I could stretch and be grateful "in all things," but even that was many times too hard. But "thankful for?" As I experienced the sweet touch of God in my life I began to see that He truly is worthy of all praise. And, I began to thank Him. As I did so, the light flooded into the windows of my soul and began the long process of detoxing my life." The most exhilarating spiritual discipline is gratitude. We live in an environment of thankfulness that focuses our attention outward. Our enemy would rob us of the joy of a thankful heart. Give thanks and live.

Grasping God's grace is more than a passive recognition of His goodness. It is far more than stoically accepting a limited season. It even exceeds standing on the promises. It is the active pursuit of God's purpose in a time that often feels aimless. Truly it is presenting our bodies, minds and spirits for the use of an almighty God to will and work through us—in season and out. Grace gives us balance in times of imbalance. Grace gives us traction in times of friction. Hamilton McHugh poignantly captures the power of grace in our lives:

Were it not for Grace, I can tell you where I'd be.
Wandering down some pointless road to nowhere

With my salvation up to me.
I know how that would go, the battles I would face.
Forever running, but losing the race;
Were it not for Grace.

Running the race with grace keeps our feet on the ground and our eyes on the goal.

REFLECTION

Getting A Foothold

1. To stay standing in life's confinements requires falling at His feet.
2. Perfection is a myth that leads to missed opportunities.
3. God wants us to see the good in a bad situation.
4. Grace and faithworks keep us standing.

Gaining Ground

1. How do I face my imperfections with grace?
2. What do I see as a "have to" that is really a "get to?"
3. What is the difference between responsiveness and responsibility?
4. When did I last laugh out loud?
5. Where do I struggle the most to stay disciplined?

REFLECTION

Following His Footsteps

Dear Father,_____

_____

_____

_____

_____

_____

_____

_____

_____Amen

MUSINGS & AMUSINGS

"Failed Again"

"If you don't like the way I do things just go find another place to live!" The angry words just rolled out of my soul, simultaneously desperate for release and comfort. I didn't want to be the responsible one—I wanted somebody to take care of me. When Dad and Mom moved in I excitedly built a nest for them, recreating a home environment and hanging all of their familiar pictures. This was going to be fun, I thought. I could bring meaning and quality to their years of declining health. What had gone wrong? Where did this anger come from? How did a cherished daughter turn into a screaming, disrespectful shrew?

In the hours that followed I quickly reviewed wise counsel from friends who had journeyed before me. "Ask for forgiveness quickly, receive it and keep moving. Don't let the enemy drive wedges between you." "Everyone is tired, scared, and frustrated...They don't like being old and sick anymore than you like them to be that way." "Perfectionism is pure fantasy in the world of caregiving."

Recovery was longer this time, but peace finally came. I had injured and wounded someone I dearly loved. I had taken precious hours at the end of his life and created havoc...I couldn't restore this lost time. But I also recognized the need to step away and hear the quiet voice of Jesus saying, "They are mine, as are you...rest."

MUSINGS & AMUSINGS

"You Just Have To Laugh"

Enduring the indignities of old age is quite an art. Maintaining modesty while strange hands examine your "uttermost parts of the earth" requires mental discipline, and a sense of humor. Dialysis three times a week keeps Dad alive after his kidney failure. He bravely, if not always cheerfully, submits to his giant washing machine. He has created a sense of community at the clinic and is engaged in the lives of both staff and other patients. His dignity is unbowed, but often tested. The man who used to be affectionately known as Fat Fred is now svelte and down right skinny. His sartorial habits haven't kept up with his weight loss, so he has adopted the chic baggy look. Recently, we made our way through the going home ritual: out of the dialysis chair, into the wheelchair, onto the scale, out of the wheelchair and into the car. In the final lap he stood to move from wheelchair to car seat and felt a sudden rush of air. As we both stood staring we realized that my high profile father was in front of the dialysis clinic with nothing but a shirt and a diaper—his pants were on the ground around his ankles. Dad immediately went from dignified to stupefied! He has always said, "What you cry about today you will laugh about tomorrow"...well tomorrow came quickly, for there was nothing we could both do but laugh. And laugh we did, until the tension of the experience melted into humor of the moment.

MUSINGS & AMUSINGS

"O'Henry Hits Home"

Remember the O'Henry story in which the adoring, but penniless young couple makes tremendous sacrifices to offer a present to the other? She sells her treasured tresses to buy a chain for his watch; he sells his watch to buy combs for her hair. Irony at its best. Dad fell asleep in his chair and was sleeping so peacefully that I couldn't bear to wake him even though it meant staying awake. As morning came he asked me if I had a good night's sleep. What? "I stayed awake so that you could sleep." "No, I stayed in my chair so that you could sleep and not have to put me to bed." O'Henry lives on. Often the concept of sacrifice becomes skewed in the heat of caregiving. Expectations and promises get twisted into a grotesque sculpture of needs and wants. What I want to do for you and what you want become confused. The elderly person wants to be useful; the caregiver wants control. Loving sacrifice becomes stoic martyrdom. The Golden Rule says that we are to do unto others as we would have them do unto us. The Platinum Rule takes the next step—do unto others as they would be done unto. Caring means considering, not controlling. True sacrifice is in humility, not tyranny.

Five Footholds For Seasons of Limitation

- **DEPEND ON GOD**
- **ACKNOWLEDGE THE REALITY**
- **GRASP GOD'S GRACE**
- **WORK WITH A NET...WORK**
- **MAKE IT COUNT**

"Rise up, this matter is in your hands. We will support you, so take courage and do it."
Ezra 10:4 (New International Version)

"Blest be the tie that binds our hearts in Christian love; The fellowship of kindred minds is like to that above. Before Our Father's throne we pour our ardent prayers; Our fears, our hopes, our aims are one, Our comforts and our cares."
John Fawcett

5

WORK WITH A NET...WORK

Networks are nets that work.

Amanda's picture was prominently displayed as the conference keynote speaker and honored guest. Her corporate rise was attributed to her Ivy League education and well-organized network. She was a woman with title, perks and high six-figure income. Magazines wrote of her and awarded her for making her mark while making a way for other women. Soon after the birth of her son she decided to resign and join the growing number of stay-at-home Moms. "Brenda, this was my decision. I looked at every alternative and chose this one. I built spreadsheets to compare the plans and this one was by far the best. But one year later I am feeling trapped." She has stepped out to make a life change and now questions if the climb up the corporate ladder wasn't easier than the climb up to the narrow precipice of stay-at-home Mom.

God's River Hogs

Logs moving down the river to the mill tend to impede the water flow by jamming up. Were they to stay stuck all forward progress would stop. Agile, courageous men stand astride the logs with long poles prepared to both prevent and break up the log locks. They are called river hogs. In confinement we often feel the sense that movement has ceased even when we are convinced that the direction of the flow is correct. We all need river hogs to skillfully release the stoppage...God river hogs.

These bold loggers probably wouldn't think of themselves as diagnosticians, but that is exactly what they are. They objectively view the situation, find the key log and apply the correct pressure to achieve release and flow. Getting unstuck in a limited situation calls for helpers who can look at our situation, assess the needs, create an approach and then line up the people to get it done. What would Amanda need to start moving again?

A SWOT analysis: what are her strengths, her weaknesses, her opportunities and her threats; how can she build a SWOT team to enhance strengths, bolster weaknesses, maximize opportunities and neutralize threats?

An objective view of the circumstances: choosing to stay home because it was best for her family goals; moving away from her career path requires a transition period and establishing new social patterns; recognizing that our identities are often aligned with our professional status and major shifts can cause emotional earthquakes.

A clear understanding of moving from Wall Street to Sesame Street: creating a network of other women for support and mental stimulation; establishing a church community to provide nurturing and spiritual guidance; adopting a mission statement that expresses the purpose of this decision; scheduling frequent checkups to measure the progress.

Flying High in Confinement

Our seasons of confinement may leave us feeling like a participant in an extreme sports segment in which we are pulled high above the circus ring to be the "daring young man/woman on the flying trapeze." How exciting it looks when we watch others. But how would you feel if suddenly you were placed on a 3 x 3 board with instructions to let go? When limitations come our lives are situated on small, exposed platforms with no place to go but into mid-air—or so it seems!

Bonnie Tsui was inspired by her flying exploits to write a piece entitled "The Trapeze Revival." She eloquently describes her sensation of climbing to the platform, getting balanced and then hearing the command "Hep" which is the action word in trapeze. It means that the flyer is getting ready to change positions. When we look back on our lives we can recognize that God called out "hep," but we just didn't know that a change was about to occur. Lili Gaudreau addresses the question of safety: "The possibility for injury is not in the air, it's in the landing." "As you drop from the trapeze swing onto the net, it's the responsibility of the person holding the safety lines below to control your fall, so you don't twist your ankle or your neck from landing in a bad position."

The parallels are stunning. As we stand on our platforms we know that something is going to change. As we let go we are dependent not only on God's sustaining hand, but also on the net(work) that provides safety and security. Our word is "Help," not Hep. Pretending to be a Flying Wollenda in life's limited times is egotistical and dangerous. Midair collisions create havoc because we have detached the safety lines and even put down the net. Henri Nouwen has been widely quoted on an experience he had with a German trapeze company. He writes of the lessons that they taught him, especially about the roles of the flyer and the catcher. The flyer is the one poised to leap at the sound of "hep." The catcher is trained to support all the weight of the flyer. Every seasoned trapezee knows that the flyer makes no effort to reach for the catcher. Instead the flyer's job is to let go and wait for the catcher's strong grip that provides the safe transfer. When God calls "hep," we must call "help."

In the late 1980s I worked as a recruiter for one of the premier firms of the Northwestern Mutual Insurance Company. The distinguished general agent was R. Allen Angell, CLU,ChFC. As he built development plans for new agents he would often say to the management team, "We need to hep the boy!" In Texas-talk this meant finding a way to help them succeed. Ironically he was using trapeze lingo, as well, for he was communicating that it was time for the agent to change positions. It was time to shift from activity and habit patterns that were not working to those that would accomplish the goals. Al was saying that helping them meant signaling that change was about to take place.

H.E.L.P.E.R.s

In our seasons of change there are three "catchers" that stabilize us as we stand on the platform with shaky knees and wobbling feet: people, programs and prayer. They signify that we are shifting by offering H.E.L.P.—Hands-on Encouragement for Life's Potholes. Asking for help is difficult for most of us. Offering to be the catcher feels so much better. But it can become a control issue—a power position. God puts us into times of confinement for our refinement and realignment.

Catcher # 1 - PEOPLE

A Network of Support

John Maxwell articulates the Law of Mount Everest: "As the challenges escalate, the need for teamwork elevates." As we reach for Hands-on Encouragement for Life's Potholes (HELP) we purposefully weave a net of competent support that provides flexibility and room for growth. Whether it is a people network, a program or a team of intercessory prayer warriors we benefit from recognizing and assembling a team that will see us through. It is important to recognize that this team is organized for a specific purpose and is not necessarily a group constructed as lifetime friendships. To plant the feet solidly on Mount Everest's peak, even the most advanced climber depends on the life-saving skills of the shirpahs. But once the ascent and descent are successfully completed there is no more reliance. We, too, will have special team members who are there for a season.

As we draw our supporters together we look for skill, spiritual development and maturity. We want to construct a support network that exemplifies Elton Trueblood's "company of the committed." These people are super-glued together so that they stick tight as long as they are on the team. Just as God ushers us into these seasons He makes a way for all the resources that will be needed. He doesn't bring us this far to leave us alone. Never are the words, "I will never leave you nor forsake you" more warmly received than in confinement. He is the great Provider (Jehovah-Jireh) who will weave the strands together and infuse it with "power from above"—the power of Biblical encouragement.

Biblical Encouragers

What exactly is biblical encouragement? It speaks God's truth in a clear, pointed and targeted way to strengthen the spirit and heart. True encouragement is focused on specific areas much like weight training is designed for particular muscle groups. It is not broad brushed but finely tuned. Encouragers are trained by the Holy Spirit to follow Paul's injunction: "Dear brothers, warn those who are lazy; comfort those who are frightened; take tender care of those who are weak; and be patient with everyone." (1 Thessalonians 5:14–The Living Bible) These marching orders identify four different forms of strengthening tailored to the specific needs. The idle, non-workers are to be warned; the frightened are to be given a sense of security; the weak are to be gently nurtured and all are to be treated with patience and forbearance. Warning, comfort, tender care and patience—four very different actions but all forms of encouragement. You see, Biblical encouragement puts many bullets into the gun. Particularly in confinement we need a team with a well-developed repertoire of actions. The task is often daunting and we will need a word of strength that speaks directly to the source of discouragement.

I believe that one of God's goals is to bring us through with a greater knowledge of Who He is and who we aren't. He wants us to understand dependence on Him, on His grace and on His people. Joshua led his people from one distinct season of confinement into the Promised Land with the oft-repeated words, "Be bold and of good courage." We can temporarily benefit from random kindnesses and hugs. But when living in a box "have a nice day," and empty "I'll be praying for you" just isn't enough. We need to have a purposeful, intentional web of catchers who know what they are doing and are committed to partnering with us. They wear the name of the Lord and enable us to "rise up and stand firm." (Psalm 20:8)

Weaving A Net

Let's explore three ways that people can provide a support net: a personal board, an apt word and skillful ministry.

Personal Boards

Chuck and Suzanna's family was known for practical jokes, effervescent laughter and love that overflowed to all around them. Their three children ranged from high school junior to middle elementary. Chuck's successful career allowed them a comfortable lifestyle that was shared with many in their church and community. Family vacations took them hiking, canoeing and rock climbing. How they loved to be together. Everything changed in an instant as three of the children watched him slip off the mountain and plunge to his death. "This just couldn't be happening to us," she said. He had lost his footing and lost his life. She knew that her children would depend on her and she surrounded herself with encouragers...not just happy-talk people. She constructed a board that would help her face the imminent business, emotional and spiritual potholes ahead. Suzanna's board represents four leadership styles that bring texture and color to a difficult problem. They represent encouragement by design. The members are well-trained, skilled and spiritually mature. Each understands what true Biblical encouragement is. They have accepted the challenge of standing with Suzanna in a critical confinement.

Suzanna, the Strategist

Suzanna is a fiery woman with high drive who values competence in herself and others. As the chairperson of community organizations she listens somewhat impatiently to proposals and then wants to know the "why" of the project. She sees way beyond the present and sees how decisions impact the organization. Chuck, as her harmonious people-centered husband, was often perceived as the damage control unit of their marriage. "I follow around behind telling people that she really didn't mean it like it sounded. I smooth feathers that she ruffles." After his death she became so much more aware of his loving counterbalance. In building her personal board she was clear about the leadership skills that would complement her own. She asked them to serve for three years knowing that confinement is for a season. In the stress of her widowhood she fights the tendency to become critical of herself and all those around her. In order to keep a grip she holds the reins too tightly assuming control of issues that are not important and not even interesting to her. Organizing a board frees her to do what she alone can do—and what she can do best. She can treat this experience as an experiment and objectively create a strategy to hold her footing. Stepping outside the experience gives her the energy to make her way through. "If I stopped to wallow in my situation I would lose all ability to function. I have to look at it from a third party perspective."

Constance, the Logistical Leader

Constance is a financial officer for a national consulting firm. She is well-known for her incisive thinking and her attention to detail. Suzanna invited her to be a tactical member who would know how to marshall the necessary resources through the next three years. "I am the traditionalist who understands the work ethic. Hard work is important to me and I want to be known by my high standards. Suzanna put me on the board to hold the course and to bring her back to center when the situation is overwhelming. She can make the plan but she looks to me to figure what we need to make it work. I know myself well and protect against being rigid, but I have a tendency to take a darker view of the future, so I am grateful for the other team members who bring a strong optimistic outlook to our board."

John, the Tactician

John is Vice President of Sales for a large manufacturing company. As a young boy he was fascinated by how things worked and was often the source of parental frustration as he dismantled the household appliances. From childhood he always created fun for everyone around him. "Let's do it now and let's have fun" has been his lifetime motto. Although he draws people to him through his charming style he isn't truly people focused. In his mind Starbucks was designed just for him—it is an experience to drink coffee. His organization knows that he is the action man who does things well, but not because he goes "by the book." His energies are directed toward his own passions and he gets really good at what he enjoys. "Suzanna needs someone to be right here and now with her. The future is important, but she will only get there one step at a time. Chuck was my best friend and I know how much he would want her to laugh. I am glad that Constance is on the team because I know that I can over commit and I wouldn't want to create chaos for Suz. She trusts me to bring a tangible focus to her situation and to get her there with a happy heart."

Jim, the Diplomat

Jim is a pastoral counselor at Suzanna's church. He has a deep love for the Lord and His people. He brings consensus and harmony to his environment and lives to help others find their personal meaning in life. She made her first call to him because she needed the diplomat who buffered her direct style. He would never replace Chuck, but he could give her wisdom and leadership as she worked to regain emotional traction. "When I received the call telling me about Chuck's death I was struck with the enormous task that lay ahead of Suzanna. She is now a single parent with impressionable children who need to know that God is real and hasn't made a mistake. Frankly, I was surprised that she asked me to sit on this board because I don't have high visibility or business credentials. I learned a long time ago that under pressure I tend to internalize and personalize a bit too much. Suzanna's logical approach, even under fire, is helpful for me. But I know that I have a great contribution to make because this season is people-centered. I appreciate my gift of looking at decisions through the impact on people. This will be important during these three years."

How can this board encourage Suzanna? First, they can bring their skills to the table that will help her practically face the box in which she now resides. She is a butterfly wrapped in a cocoon. They will stay with her until she emerges in all of her bright coloration and broad wings to take flight. Next, they can keep her eyes focused on the goal without neglecting the emotional nature of this time. A balanced board will give her the freedom to have someone to cry with and someone to whom she can be accountable. We need both. Finally, they will know that her specific core value is competence and work hard to build her up in recognizing areas of strength. When they operate well as a board they encourage her. After I discussed the footholds with her and talked about encouragement languages Constance remarked that she saw Suzanna's face light up as she commented on the well-organized plan for her personal period of limitation. "She acknowledges her reality and daily renews her dependence on God. She feels the irrepressible flow of grace in her life and she immerses others in her awe of God. She does it well. I enjoy strengthening her heart and giving her courage as I know her better and speak her encouragement language."

An Apt Word

Aroma of Love

Scripture tells us that we are all to encourage one another. The writer to Hebrews implores us to "Encourage one another while it is still called today." (Hebrews 3:13–New International Version) There is an urgency in that injunction. Often a well-worded statement is the key to the heart. When my Mom died I got a call from my three year old grandson, Colby, who earnestly said, "Gram, I wrote you a note of encouragement." During this extremely painful time he gave me boldness and courage…he truly encouraged me. A friend in Canada sends flowers to our house every Monday. This first started after a visit and a quick conversation with Mom about her love for flowers. The first bouquet arrived—and then the next—and then the next. For over four years the "aroma of friendship" has filled the house. When the doorbell rang on Mondays Mom would brighten up, knowing that "the flowers are here!" Each floral arrangement is accompanied by a personally composed note that expresses hope for the week and rejoicing for God's goodness.

First Baptist Church of Nashville, Tennessee sponsored a group of women who met weekly to scan the newspaper and write notes of encouragement to those who were confined by tragedy. The Headliners carefully sifted through articles and prayerfully composed letters of hope and concern. Their words brought His Word to emotional prisons often using these brief expressions to break through the darkness and shine the light of His presence into their hearts. Moms-in-Touch pray faithfully for the teachers and administrators of their children's schools. A high school math teacher tearfully related the joy that she found in knowing that Moms were actively praying for her as she fought through the trials of a difficult school year.

E-mail and written communication can facilitate the gift of encouragement. Seasons of house arrest cry out for contact with the "outside world." Faithful partners can bring the fresh air of friendship and encouragement. Dad's incapacity limits him to bed. Hundreds of e-mails have been received that thank him for stretching them. "I will never meet you this side of heaven but I want you to know that you have made a difference in my life," wrote a man from Guatemala. He has learned Dad's language and speaks courage to his heart. "An apt word is like apples of silver in settings of silver." (Proverbs 25:11–New International Version) In times of limitation create a system of communication that will open the door to the prison. Choose the words wisely and aim the arrow like a heat-seeking missile.

Hope For The Hopeless

I sat in the narrow waiting room not-so-patiently clock watching as Dad underwent hours of a doctor-ordered scan. He was carefully balanced on a thin board while a machine searched for traces of the melanoma that had invaded his body. The intricate mechanism hummed and I groaned. The woman directly across from me tried, in vain, to engage me in light conversation. I was definitely not interested. I was armed for word war—my laptop was in place and I was going to spend three hours writing about caring and compassion during times of confinement! Finally, her voice broke through my hard shell and I realized that she needed to talk. Her husband was undergoing scans to determine if the last round of chemotherapy had been successful. I glibly mentioned that I was writing a book on confinement and limitation. "Do those words resonate with you?" Her story just poured out of her and we spent the next two hours sharing about the presence of God when we are under "house arrest." She knew that his season was coming to an end and that she was facing a new season without him. Her demeanor was one of dependence and her wisdom was gained through a careful walk with the Lord. How much she had to teach me that day.

I asked her about encouragement and she told me of a visit her husband had made to a bed-ridden friend with a demanding spirit. "Don't expect everyone to stop and wait on you. Be grateful and do whatever you can for yourself." She said that in love he had spoken directly to his friend whose grief had turned him into a complainer who was exhausting his family. Encouragement can be tough-minded. There is nothing cowardly about courageously emboldening another. A Biblical encourager has to have tremendous backbone and be willing to know that "no" is an encouraging word. "Where seldom is heard a discouraging word" is great for the range, but it fails in the Body of Christ. We would be overrun with weak-willed, preying coyotes if we did that.

Skillful Ministry

My good friend, Ruth Grimm, has served as God's encourager for many enduring severe confinements even as she suffers from physical disabilities that limit her activities and cause her great pain. She was asked to give some practical advice on ministering to the sick and dying. With her generous permission I am reprinting her notes. It is a superb primer.

Ministering to the Sick, Elderly, Dying

- Allow people who are experiencing declining physical ability to do as much as possible for themselves (unless dangerous). Patterns from a lifetime of independence cannot automatically be turned off from the mind.

- Keep in mind that the journey can be quite frightening—they have not been this way before either.

- Company on a lonely journey is always better. Don't avoid talking with them about heaven/death. It's on their minds anyway.

- Remember that the elderly, ill or dying person does not have a physical way to "work" off frustrations that he is dealing with. Allow for "bad attitudes."

- Be aware that depression and frustration stem from having to depend on others.

- When visiting at hospital or at home, avoid making conversation with other visitors to the exclusion of the one being visited.

- Listen, rather than doing all the talking.

- Keep visits short and sweet unless you are a primary caretaker.

- Avoid assuming that you automatically know what is best for the sick/elderly/dying one. They often know much better.

- Encourage the elderly to talk about their lives and the past if they are not too weak. Recalling a time when they were not feeling quite so useless can lift spirits.

- Remind them, in words or writing, how much they have meant to you or others in some specific way.

- If you sense they are "bottling up," verbalize their pain/frustration/anxiety for them occasionally—in order that they understand that you understand how they are feeling.

- Respect their dignity as much as is possible.

- Resist "talking down" to a person in declining health. Wheelchairs do not necessarily take off IQ points, and it will cause further depression to the suffering one.

- Expect some confusion in the elderly or heavily-medicated when they are transferring back and forth between hospital and home. Reminding them often of their whereabouts can be reassuring.

- Use discretion in quoting scripture. Romans 8:28 given to someone wrestling with raw emotions can seem like a scolding. The verses 38 & 39 that end that same chapter, on the other hand, can be quite uplifting and full of hope.

- A favorite hymn of theirs sung or played, or a favorite scripture can be an encouragement to one who doesn't feel up to singing or reading scripture.

- Make an effort to view things through their eyes—identify with them if possible, just like we seek to do with our children.

- Don't "intrude" or "insist" except where necessary. Learn to "read" responses and body language.

- Anticipate, anticipate, anticipate! Whenever possible, offer a specific service rather than asking if there is anything you can do. "Yes" or "No" takes less energy.

- If they've been used to keeping a checkbook, be sure they know that a specific person is handling their finances well.

- At a time when they are feeling rather "unlovely," touching is extremely important: hugs, holding a hand, caressing in some way.

- Assure them they are being prayed for, or name a specific time or place that they were prayed for. They may be too ill or confused to pray for themselves.

- Praying aloud with them can be extremely comforting—just the sound of a friend or loved one voicing petitions on their behalf.

- Be aware that a great deal of bonding takes place while caring for the dying—and in the midst of the busyness, one can be quite unprepared for the parting that comes with death.

- Be aware that ministering to the sick and dying can get to be an "all-encompassing" thing and can quickly become "our reason for being"!

- No one of us can expect to be all things to the suffering one, nor should we try to be. Remember that God has his network in place within the body of believers, God will clearly show us "who" and "when," as well as what our responsibilities should be. A prideful spirit can develop in the ministering one if others are not also involved.

- Their "valley" has probably brought them into an ever more intimate relationship with their Savior if they are believers. BE PREPARED TO BE BLESSED! They may have many thoughts and words of wisdom!

People are the first catcher as we launch into a season of confinement. An effective webbing of family and friends creates the best kind of networks—nets that work. The Preacher saw the pragmatism of shared experiences when he wrote, "Two can accomplish more than twice as much as one, for the results can be much better. If one falls, the other pulls him up, but if a man falls when he is alone, he's in trouble...And one standing alone can be attacked and defeated, but two can stand back-to-back and conquer; three is even better, for a triple-braided cord is not easily broken." (Ecclesiastes 4: 9-11–The Living Bible) The people of God are our first line of defense when He lovingly confines us to melt and mold.

Catcher # 2 - PROGRAMS

Supporting One Another

A well-defined support group is an effective way of achieving hands-on encouragement. Caroline escaped the terror of an abusive husband without the needed structure to rebuild her life. A friend at work invited her to a church group that was designed to help others climb out of life's potholes. "I didn't want to go. It was really hard to admit to others that I needed help. For the first few months I sat quietly in the back listening to the others share stories of addiction, compulsion and destruction. I started thinking that maybe I didn't belong. Slowly, I started seeing that I didn't have an addictive personality—I was an addict. I was addicted to pain and I needed help. They are now my life-line and I am so thankful to the Lord for bringing them into my life."

Finding the right support group means identifying the need to be satisfied. Is this an informational network that provides educational and skill-building tools? For example, is this a program that retrains for new jobs? Or, is this a network of people who have experienced the same confinement?

Lynne Kinghorn, PhD in her excellent article, "Feeling Home-Alone? 15 Ways to Combat This Common Complaint" recommends a support group for mothers-at-home. "This is one of the absolute best ways to decrease your loneliness and gain support for your lifestyle. You can meet weekly and talk while the children play, if that works for you. One enterprising group hires a sitter to keep track of the kids at one home so they actually have uninterrupted talk time. A really good group is one in which differing opinions are respected, each member gets her fair share of "air time" and there is a genuine sense of mutual support."

Amanda was invited to attend a MOPS (Mothers of Pre-Schoolers) meeting in her neighborhood and immediately found women who had chosen to trade corporate and professional careers for full-time mothering. One website testimonial says it this way,

> *"What MOPS has provided for me... is a welcome break; a chance to make new friends; the opportunity to know I'm not the only mom who goes through the struggles and joys of raising young children..."*

In her local group she found Moms who shared common experiences. They were walking and talking together. Without this bond, the situation often becomes bondage.

Common Cares

Charla heard those dreaded words, "The results are back and it is cancer." Her season of confinement began with that phone call. Each trip to the oncology clinic triggered new questions and new fears. Her children were grown and her husband traveled 40% of the time. Her new friends from the cancer support group enabled her to function in her "new normal" mode. The monthly meetings and weekly coffees "give me a safe place to be real. I don't have to be afraid to share. Nobody runs away from the fear that becomes the elephant in the room for so many. We see it, name it and help each other to deal with it. We are convinced that cancer is not an automatic death sentence. It is something that we learn to live with!"

After 15 years of interning and working as a valued assistant, Josh felt the pressure of financial confinement as he mortgaged his house and tightened the family budget to start his own graphic arts studio. Janet, his wife of 12 years, believed in his dream and committed herself to supporting him. She was his primary encourager, but he also knew that a professional organization would help fill in the holes he had in his business experience. He had read of the high mortality rate for start-up businesses and he wanted to beat the odds. SCORE (Service Corps of Retired Executives) provided a network of highly seasoned men and women who were giving back to the next generation through free consulting services. "I did not know that having a dream was merely a babystep in establishing a profitable, sustainable studio. I took a lot for granted when I was the employee and not the boss. Working for myself means working twice as hard. SCORE gave me the information and support that I needed to understand how to build a business plan, set reasonable goals and measure my achievements. They gave me a track to run on when all I had was enthusiasm, energy and lots of desire."

A news release about an entrepreneurial encouragement support group in Swain County (North Carolina) announced that a program, conceived by the Partnership for the Future of Bryson City and Swain County, would "encapsulate entrepreneurs in a support network, help them grow their businesses into viable enterprises, and then spin them out of the encapsulation to survive on their own. "I and several other entrepreneurial friends have spent a number of years discussing ways to truly assist people with growing profitable, sustainable small businesses," said Bill Schutters, director of the Partnership. Three key ingredients include financial backing, product development and good marketing. The program would help the entrepreneurs with these business components through a network of mentors, using the slogan "entrepreneurship by entrepreneurs for entrepreneurs."

Catcher # 3 -PRAYER

Together Before The Throne

Praying for one another is a biblical imperative and spiritual privilege. Participating in the sufferings of one another allows us a close up and personal view of God's working. It is impossible to pray fervently for someone and not stay connected. Friends of mine are missionaries in a dangerous Middle Eastern country. Each day they send an email journal entry to a list of praying friends. Repeatedly they relate stories of God's providence and care. Without fail, they say, "Thank you for praying—we know that you are here with us." Their lives are in jeopardy; our hearts are joined together through intercessory prayer.

In 1861 Charles Haddon Spurgeon commented on intercession with beautifully crafted phrases birthed from a heart of worship:

> I commend the blessed privilege of intercession, because of its sweet brotherly nature. You and I may be naturally hard, and harsh, and unlovely of spirit, but praying much for others will remind us we have, indeed, a relationship to the saints, that their interests are ours, that we are jointly concerned with them in all the privileges of grace. I do not know anything which, through the grace of God, may be a better means of uniting us the one to the other than constant prayer for each other. First, remember that intercessory prayer is the sweetest prayer God ever hears. Do not question it, for the prayer of Christ is of this character. In all the incense which now our Great High Priest puts into the censer, there is not a single grain that is for himself. His work is done; his reward obtained. Now you do not doubt but that Christ's prayer is the most acceptable of all supplications. Very well, my brethren, the more like your prayer is to Christ's, the more sweet it will be; and while petitions for yourself will be accepted, yet your pleadings for others, having in them more of the fruits of the Spirit, more love, perhaps more faith, certainly more brotherly kindness, they will be as the sweetest oblation that you can offer to God, the very fat of thy sacrifice.

Seasons of Intercession

The old hymn, Sweet Hour of Prayer, speaks of "seasons of despair and grief" and the ensuing relief that comes through prayer. Intercessors stand in the gap for those in these seasons and share the relief that is provided. No, we don't understand the process, but we see the blessed out workings of interceding. Paul's prayers on behalf of his "children in Christ" continue to stir us as we read them. How can we not be profoundly moved as he asks the Father to give the believers at Ephesus the power "to grasp how wide and long and high and deep is the love of Christ?" Is there any season that can extend beyond those parameters? Indeed there is not.

Exodus 28 describes the garments designed by God for Aaron. On the breast piece were 12 jewels representing the 12 tribes of Israel. When they performed their duties they were carrying a representation of those for whom they were praying. "Whenever Aaron enters the Holy Place, he will bear the names of the sons of Israel over his heart on the breast piece of decision as a continuing memorial before the Lord."

When we go before the Lord in prayer for one another we are serving a priestly function and we wear the names of those whom we remember. They are "precious jewels" embroidered upon our breasts. We carry them in our hearts and stand with them before God on their behalf. Just as our Lord stands in for us, we are "in the stead" of others. The breast piece of decision is a reminder to us of the sacred privilege we have taken up in warring before the Lord for His children. Aaron specifically bore the insignia of the 12 tribes; we bear the names and burdens of those we love. The breast piece for Aaron represented the tribes; the breast piece for us represents the tributes. "Before our Father's throne we pour our ardent prayers; our fears, our hopes, our aims are one, our comforts and our cares."

The Power of Prayer

Harold Myra, CEO of Christianity Today, Inc. frames the power of prayer this way: "In his book, *Life Can Begin Again,* Thielicke says during the worst time of persecution, he stood up for Christ and then was able to say joyfully, almost exultantly, 'I'm through. I've made it. Now what comes of it is God's responsibility. Now I have summoned God into the fray...God himself rises up to perform his mighty works in the midst of the earth, where the powers clash and the terrible battle rages.'

Our prayers summon God into the fray. Our listening for the whisper of the Spirit leads us through tangled and thorny thickets. We are called to have ears to hear and eyes to see."

Catchers Are Keepers

Healthy communities grow skilled, alert catchers. When we are perched on the tiny platform it seems like the entire world is watching. The trapeze bar swings toward us; we feel that we are pushed into mid-air. As the wind rushes into our face we are caught up in the sheer fright of the experience, but exhilarated as we anticipate the strength of the catcher who reaches out to support us. "Don't do anything—just let go." Those words of the trainer ring over and over. But all of our survival instincts make us want to reach frantically for the catcher. However, he catches our eyes before he catches our hands and calms us. "Just let go and let the catcher do his work—he will support you." In seasons of confinement we are hanging out for the entire world to see. Our technique is usually amateurish and our screams can often be heard beyond the cacophony of the confusion around us. But we look and see that God has provided catchers to give encouragement: people, programs and prayer. They are strong, well-skilled and capable of bringing us safely to the other side. Once our feet hit the platform, we can take a breath and see that the flyer is truly along for the ride—the ride of a lifetime!

Over the last three years Dad's death has been "imminent" at least four times. The complex web of prayer partners astounds me, but praise wells up in awe-ful gratitude for the magnificent connectivity of intercessory prayer long before the internet was ever imagined. Instead of Musings and Amusings about Caregiving I want to share excerpts from daily health updates on the website breakfastwithfred.com during Dad's hospitalization. Through God's kindness Dad recovered. "I don't understand intercessory prayer, but I just know it works," he says.

March 24

Fred Smith is in the hospital with a staph infection in his hip. He has been heavily medicated and has undergone two dialysis treatments to keep the fluid level in range. He woke up this morning experiencing less pain than before. He has been alert and able to talk with the medical staff. I mentioned that lots of people are praying and he replied, "That is why I am still here." He is most thankful, as is the entire Smith family. He is having a catheter inserted into the hip to drain accumulating fluid. Also, an infectious disease specialist will be seeing him today. He is amazingly strong and works to bless all around him, even when he is in tremendous pain.

Thanks for praying. You can check in for updates.

April 3

Fred is nearing the end of his earthly work. Please pray for his peace and comfort as he finishes well. Pray for his wife, Mary Alice that she will continue to experience God's mercy, grace and love.

Thank you for your intercession. Fred's desire was to be helpful and to stretch others. We know that the Lord has stretched you as you have prayed. May Jesus Christ Be Praised!

April 13

Last Saturday we were told that he would most assuredly be in heaven on this Resurrection Sunday but God certainly has His own timing. His favorite nurse, Maggie, from the outpatient dialysis center came for a visit. When she was leaving she reminded him that he wouldn't go until God called the game.

Please pray that the doctors will comprehend that Fred is prepared to die, but not wanting to die. They have rarely seen someone with his physical deterioration who has such a strong mind and spirit. Our continuing prayer is that the witness of Fred, friends and family will lift up the name of Jesus. That in all we do and say He will be honored.

Fred knows that you are praying and he wanted you all to know yesterday that he feels your prayers and he sees the effects of the fervent intercession. He said that it isn't the numbers that matter to God but that the hearts are ones of love for him and for our Lord.

Thank you and May Jesus Christ Be Praised.

April 21

When was the last time eating a bowl of oatmeal and drinking a large glass of apple juice was considered a memorable event? Seeing Fred sit up and eat real food was a milestone! The feeding tube is gone, as is the oxygen mask and other miscellaneous "tubery." Tomorrow is still the scheduled departure date. He is eager to get home and out of the reach of any and all who would like to get their hands on his body. When his brother Joe mentioned today that there must still be work to do he mused that perhaps it was seeing just how much medical treatment he could take. When Joe suggested that perhaps he would be given some ink in a medical journal he simply smirked.

Shaving is the Fred story for today: the nurses are continually frustrated by his unwillingness to let them shave his 30 day growth. He explained that it is the only option he has left under his control and he is going to exercise his power to say no to shaving.

Our daily journey may end soon, but our heartfelt thanks will ever be yours. Thanks for the emails, the calls, the cards and the ongoing expressions of love and faith. It is our prayer that throughout this month your prayer life has become strengthened, your life blessed and your heart strangely warmed by the participation in Fred's story. Each of you is an important piece.

All glory, honor and praise to the God and Father of us all. And eternal and everlasting worship to Jesus Christ our Lord.

April 23

Daily updates will now transition back to weekly and then monthly, but you just have to have this last one.

Remember the "saying no to shaving is my only option and I am going to exercise it, so get away from me with that razor" Fred? Well, he had decided that he would not shave until he came home. *Today is the day to go from grizzled to chiseled.*

Fred slept well, is thoroughly enjoying having things done according to his schedule, and eating food that has distinguishable qualities. The night before he came home the dinner tray had an entree described as "pork." As I fed him I seriously wondered about the texture, but said nothing until he looked up between bites and said, "Do you think this is really meat?"

I would like to say a personal word to you. In the darkest of times I knew you were there and I knew that I wanted to share the day's journey with you. You strengthened me, energized me and focused me. Thanks so very much. May you experience the blessing of God in a new and deeper way.

REFLECTION

Getting A Foothold

1. Asking for help is a step toward stability.
2. Seasons of limitation call for closely woven support nets.
3. Biblical encouragement is laser-focused, appropriately aimed and scripturally based.
4. People, programs and prayer form the three legs of support in confinement.

Gaining Ground

1. How do I build dependable "catchers"?
2. What strengthens and encourages me?
3. What would a personal board look like?
4. Who are my prayer warriors?

REFLECTION

Following His Footsteps

Dear Father,_____

_____

_____

_____

_____

_____

_____

_____

_____Amen

Five Footholds For Seasons of Limitation

- **DEPEND ON GOD**
- **ACKNOWLEDGE THE REALITY**
- **GRASP GOD'S GRACE**
- **WORK WITH A NET...WORK**
- **MAKE IT COUNT**

"What a wonderful God we have—he is the Father of our Lord Jesus Christ, the source of every mercy, and the one who so wonderfully comforts and strengthens us in our hardships and trials. And why does he do this? So that when others are troubled, needing our sympathy and encouragement, we can pass on to them this same help and comfort God has given us."
2 Corinthians 3, 4 (The Living Bible)

"Give as 'twas given to you in your need, love as the Master loved you; Be to the helpless a helper indeed, unto your mission be true. Make me a blessing, make me a blessing, out of my life may Jesus shine; Make me a blessing, O Savior, I pray. Make me a blessing to someone today."
Ira B. Wilson

6

MAKE IT COUNT

Turn your cells into celebrations!

Dad was seated on the platform at the Bill Glass Champions for Life dinner preparing to speak when he spotted a young man at the front table. His face shone so brightly that Dad couldn't miss it. There was something distinctive in his demeanor. "That is someone I want to talk to," thought Dad. In the middle of a stirring presentation about Bill's prison ministry the speaker paused and spoke directly to this young man. "George, come up here and tell the audience what I said to you when we first met. And then tell them what you said to me." He came to the microphone and told the story of meeting the speaker whose first words were, "I understand you're an ex-tough dude, an ex-con, an ex-druggie and an ex-dealer." "I am not an ex-anything," George shot back. "I am a new creature in Christ Jesus." When we are released from our seasons of confinement we are not "ex- anythings" either. We are participants in and recipients of God's grace. In a very real way, we are new creatures because we will never be the same. Our lives will be changed because He has touched us and we, in turn, will touch others. *We can turn our cells into celebrations.*

Christ's Freedom

Eleanor's eyes filled with tears as she thought back on her confinement experiences. Her reflection was personal and private so we sat quietly while her mind retraced seasons of limitation. She would randomly speak a word as if it bubbled over in her musings. When she had processed through her life she stopped and said two words—"concentration camp." Then a story unfolded of failed marriages and the failing health of herself and her only child. As she told her story I saw why her word picture was one of incarceration. She was literally left to die and through God's grace recovered. To support herself and a dangerously sick child she took any available work that was honest and decent. Where was God in all of this she often wondered? Who was the God that she had heard of in her childhood? If "Jesus loves the little children...all the children of the world," why was her daughter suffering from a debilitating disease and why couldn't she afford proper treatment? Into this heaviness God stepped through the life of Corrie Ten Boom who survived the holocaust. Imprisoned not as a Jew, but as a protector of Jewish men, women and children in Holland, she lost her family to murdering terrorists. To Eleanor her story, *The Hiding Place*, revealed Christ's freedom in the hell-holes of Nazi concentration camps. "That's it! I have been in a concentration camp, but without Jesus!" Later she was introduced to Corrie through the dramatic interpretation of Evelyn Hines, a Dallas-area actress who has dedicated herself to the artful presentation of the Dutch woman's message. When Evelyn shared the words of Corrie, Eleanor's heart was pressed down and then released. For the first time she had more than questions; she had life-giving answers. Now Eleanor was being encouraged by the petite Dallas dramatist to take the grief and the tears and make them count.

His Cross—Our Feet

"Sweetly, Lord, have we heard Thee calling, "Come follow Me!" And we see where Thy footprints falling, Lead us to Thee." Mary Slade's words resonate with the truth of all who have faced seasons of confinements. Anna wisely observed "too often we think of confinement as punishment—deserved punishment, but when I saw that it was a stop on the road to my undeserved reward from Him I changed my mind." Ray Stedman put it this way: "When I realized that God was for me it completely changed my life!" When He says, "Come, follow Me!" it is with the blessed assurance that we know He is faithful and dependable. We know that as we see His footprints we can follow in total dependence. Just as her picture of footprints leading us to Jesus is drawn, we know that our situations are ones of realizing Who He is and being granted grace to follow. Often we feel that we are out front and just hope that He is somewhere in the neighborhood. But the truth is that He is always in the lead and we can follow in confidence and security. Her last verse appropriately speaks to our pathway. "Then at last, when on high He sees us, Our journey done, We will rest where the steps of Jesus End at His throne." This is written of life's travels, but it is equally true of our seasons. There is an end to the confinement. His divine confinement has a provision for exiting. And surprisingly enough, as we close the door to this experience, we see Him seated "high and lifted up." He was there all the time and it was to bring glory to Him as well as refine us.

Comforting The Comfortless

Christmas time always reminds me of the Messiah and the Tenor's plaintive recitative: "Comfort ye, comfort ye, my people....saith your God; speak ye comfortably to Jerusalem; and cry unto her, that her warfare is accomplished, that her iniquity is pardoned. The current vernacular talks of mashed potatoes and chicken-friend steak as "comfort foods." Over-sized clothes in plushy fabrics are sneeringly referred to by fashion experts as "comfortable." What we define as an acceptable balance between risks and rewards is our "comfort zone." I have a good friend who currently is experiencing the deliciousness of falling in love. "I feel like I have known him forever. He is so comfortable to be around." And of course, a big sigh always follows the expression of bonding!

But comfort is an old-fashioned word... and a Biblical word, as well. Ruth thanked Boaz for the comfort that he gave her. David, the shepherd, remarked that his rod and staff comforted him. Friends came to Bethany to comfort Mary and Martha in their loss of brother Lazarus. Jesus came and brought ultimate comfort as He spoke to them of resurrection and everlasting life. The Lord's words through the prophet Jeremiah speak directly to the hearts of all who have endured confinement: "They will come with weeping; they will pray as I bring them back. I will lead them beside streams of water on a level path where they will not stumble...I will turn their mourning into gladness; I will give them comfort and joy instead of sorrow." (Jeremiah 31:9,13–New International Version) God makes reapers out of weepers.

In the late 18th century an unknown poet wrote of true comfort and joy: "God rest you merry, Gentlemen, let nothing you dismay, Remember Christ our Savior was born on Christmas Day, to save us all from Satan's pow'r when we were gone astray, O Tidings of comfort and joy, comfort and joy, O tidings of comfort and joy." As He unlocks us from house arrest and opens wide the holding cell we are reminded that nothing should cause us dismay. He who designed our confinement now ordains that the time is over. We may have gone out in mourning, but we come back rejoicing. He has done His work and it is time to tell of His goodness. It is time to tell of the ways He comforted us.

While most children were cradled to Rock-a-Bye-Baby we were put to sleep (as were our children and grandchildren) to the hymn, "Take The Name of Jesus With You." Mom would either hum, sing or whistle the tune. There are now three generations in our family who have been imprinted with this precious melody. At Mom's memorial service there was no doubt of our musical selection. The words speak wonderfully to the goal of this foothold: "Take the name of Jesus with you, child of sorrow and of woe; It will joy and comfort give you—Take it, then, wher-e'er you go. At the name of Jesus bowing, Falling prostrate at His feet, King of kings in heav'n we'll crown Him, When our journey is complete." When our season of limitation is complete the name of Jesus will go with us as we walk forward.

Purposeful Comfort

The Biblical tongue twister of 2nd Corinthians has deeply touched Caroline's life. "I want my life to be all about comforting others with the comfort with which He has comforted me—I want to be a Second Corinthians woman." Whew! That is a mouthful—and a heartful. What does that mean? Does it mean simply sympathizing with every person in a difficult situation? Does it only mean having a cheerful word for all? If you have read foothold #4 then you know that I believe the answer is a resounding "no way!" How did He comfort you? Caroline is quick to answer in her specific, organized and no-nonsense way.

> He gave me the hope of salvation through Jesus Christ my Lord.

> He opened the scriptures to bring peace, help, and support.

> He showed me how to structure a network of friends and family to see me through to the other side.

> He changed my thinking to create a life that wasn't dependent on experiences that would fill emotional holes; he showed me what true reality is.

> He gave me a pattern of a loving Father who disciplines because He is transforming and conforming.

He put me into a Christian fellowship that understood my goals and held me accountable.

He put a new song in my heart—a song of deliverance.

He gave me a desire to comfort others and to be a Biblical encourager.

Comfort has now moved from ancient prophet to 18th century poet to 21st century Christian woman. Her personal mission statement clearly states that she is focused on making each day of her confinement count for Christ. He was there with her, even when she didn't know or want Him. Now her life is fulfilled by reaching out to others to bring Godly strength and comfort into the healing process.

Making A Difference

Stephanie S. Sawyer is the author of *Facing Me: Breaking the Bonds of Seizure Confinement, A Journey in Faith and Restoration*. As a last effort to overcome the impact of epileptic seizures she agreed to radical surgery. Recovery encompassed all of her: physical, emotional and spiritual. She says that after surgery she had to meet and learn to know an entirely new person. Her book chronicles her challenge. She speaks of why she wrote and why she speaks boldly about seizures: "My message is twofold. I want to inspire and encourage others facing what they deem to be insurmountable obstacles. For me to allow doctors to drill holes in my skull and remove a lobe of my brain, a mind-shattering concept for any person, had to take remarkable courage. I rested completely on my Christian faith, which told me this opportunity was no coincidence. I knew that God wanted something for me far beyond my comprehension though I could not see it yet. Secondly, I wanted to encourage other sufferers of epilepsy or other neurological diseases. I pray that the general public comes to a better understanding, and develops compassion for those afflicted with seizures." She has a passion to make a difference.

But I don't think that I have met many people who didn't want to make a difference in the lives of others. Have you? Often we read of the desire for contribution. Men and women regularly drop out of high-paying, high visibility careers to work for non-profits. We are routinely challenged to become change agents in our environment. Rarely do we hear a motivational speaker who doesn't drive home the need for meaning. "I don't think I wanted to make a difference until I was confined," commented Bill as we talked about making it count. Until he faced financial reversals he had little interest in giving. But a job loss and a period of limitation sensitized him to the needs of others and to God's great provision. Is it possible that we are constrained in our giving comfort until we truly have received it? But once we are comforted are we not bound to provide it for others? Isn't the picture of two hands extended—one hand up to God and one hand out to others—the appropriate view? We, who have been given so much must then consider how to translate our season into something worthwhile.

Let's think about five steps in making it count:
1. Close the door
2. Evaluate the experience
3. Prepare an explanation for the hope that is in you
4. Watch for and act on opportunities to comfort others
5. Celebrate the goodness of God

Close The Door

Randall's candor about his unemployment was refreshing. "I know that in the high-tech business I may face this time and time again, but I certainly can't be afraid of it. I have a new job and that is where my focus will be." Often a confinement will leave us shell-shocked and constantly glancing in our emotional rear-view mirrors. By doing this we drag the experience into the next stage, but don't bring the learnings. God designs our limited circumstances to teach us specific lessons about Himself and about us. When we bring the fears and dread of repeating "life in the box" with us we discount the value of that time. "Fear not" is frequently repeated in scripture because we tend toward anxiety. When the period of unemployment ends, when the divorce decree is granted, when the doctor declares us symptom free, when the children successfully complete rehab—all these are times to close the door. "When God finishes something it must be finished," is the way Oswald Chambers expresses it. The old rock and roll song says it a little more bluntly, but gets the point across: "Hit the road, Jack, and doncha come back no more, no more!" We may face similar times in the future, but this one is over and we need to see God's sufficiency. This is a time to give thanks. Solomon painted this word picture of closing the door: "See! The winter is past; the rains are over and gone. Flowers appear on the earth; the season of singing has come." (Song of Solomon 2:11–New International Version)

A TV commercial for FedEx shows a lady in a very long post office line. She is pushing her packages along with her foot as she works her way toward the counter. The camera shifts to a smiling woman having her packages expertly wrapped by a man with an even bigger smile. She speaks the punch line, "I used to be a scooter, but now I use FedEx mailing services." All of us tend to be scooters. We carry cares and concerns with us and work our way through life scooting them ahead of us in line hoping to get to the counter and be rid of them. When we are through with a season and don't close the door we become professional scooters. We take on burdens that God hasn't given us the grace to carry. He gives us the freedom to mail the packages before saying goodbye to the confinement and walk out with empty arms and a full heart.

When we wallow in a season, our hearts become fallow and our lives become shallow. To be encouragers our hearts must be soft and fertile. Leonard Sweet, in his intriguing book *A Cup of Coffee At The Soul Cafe* describes this process as " keeping the clay moist." Hardened clay is worthless, but when it is malleable and soft it is good for shaping into vessels of usefulness. The prophet exhorts us to "plant the good seeds of righteousness and you will reap a crop of my love; plow the hard ground of your hearts, for now is the time to seek the Lord, that he may come and shower salvation upon you." (Hosea 10:12–The Living Bible) People who make it count then pour the blessings of God's salvation on others. "How beautiful upon the mountains are the feet of those who bring the happy news of peace and salvation...for the Lord has comforted His people." (Isaiah 52:7,9–The Living Bible)

Evaluate The Experience

Sue Ellen's career as a marketing manager was in high gear. She directed the branding efforts for a nationally recognized product. While taking the usual route to the office her car was violently struck by a driver whose attention was momentarily diverted, causing him to run a red light and careen into Sue Ellen's sports car. In a split second the definition of normal was turned upside down. Months of hospitalization followed. How could she be headed to a decision meeting on an advertising campaign and suddenly have her life dramatically changed? As she recovered she approached the process with an objective, business-like method. Rather than deal with what-ifs and whys she started an assessment sheet.

What were the positives?
What were the negatives?
How could she use this time to best advantage?
Who could benefit from her experience?
How had she changed through this hospitalization?
Where did she see God's direction?
Where did she see God's protection?

This personal debriefing allowed her to think back through the accident and hospitalization without bitterness but without denial. For example, she could clearly see that she had no responsibility for the crash, but she knew that forgiveness was part of her healing. She began to understand that her priorities were out of sync and the involuntary sabbatical gave her a better perspective on what really mattered. "I still love my work and am even more grateful for the opportunity to use my gifts, but I know that I don't live to work anymore."

A key element of assessment is understanding that the experience was ours, but that it was for the benefit of others, as well. In 1972 Edward Lorenz, an esteemed physicist, presented a paper and questioned, "Does the flap of a butterfly's wings in Brazil set off a tornado in Texas?" He was a researcher in chaos theory. Despite the current use of the word chaos, this scientific study refers to the apparent randomness of systems. But study has proven that all systems rely on foundational order. Some behaviors, perhaps even the flap of butterfly wings, can cause complex events to occur. As I write this, Corpus Christi, Texas is covered with 4 inches of snow—the greatest in 100 years. The Brazilian butterflies must have gotten themselves into quite a flap to cause this! Nothing we experience is for us alone. We are connected through the purposeful design of our Creator. Whether it is for the benefit of the angels, the cloud of witnesses or the neighbor next door, the confinement is ours to share.

At the close of The Hobbit Gandalf and Bilbo are having a thoughtful conversation. Bilbo thinks about his "most excellent adventure" and Gandalf responds, "You don't really suppose, do you, that all your adventures were managed by mere luck, just for your sole benefit? You are a very fine person, Mr. Baggins, and I am very fond of you; but you are only quite a little fellow in a wide world after all." "Thank goodness!" replies Bilbo. We are mysteriously linked to one another. Choosing to turn our cell into a learning lab rather than marking days off on the wall makes great sense when we grasp that we are not alone.

Prepare an Answer for the Hope

"Fred, how do you live with renal failure and dialysis?" When someone asks Dad a question like that I usually roll my eyes. What choice does he have? But then I remember that he has a clear choice—the choice of his attitude. As you know we were steeped in Viktor Frankl's idea that man cannot choose his circumstances nor even change them at times—but he had the choice of his attitude. They could strip him of everything material but they could not strip him of his human dignity. It was hard for a teenager living in an affluent suburb of Cincinnati to actually comprehend what a prison camp environment would be, but I was convinced that it was a place to "choose my attitude." As I aged, personal prisons gave me ample opportunities to make those choices. In watching Dad I know that there is more to it than just attitude, there is hope. Peter, in his first letter, considers seasons of suffering. What does he encourage the readers to do? "Always be prepared to give an answer to everyone who asks you to give the reason for the hope that you have." (1 Peter 3:15—New International Version)

My brother Fred commented that we used to find secluded phone booths, close the door and conduct our phone conversations privately. Now we stand in the middle of Starbucks and hope that everyone hears. Accordingly, we "live out loud" with everything played out in public. We rarely live in such privacy that our confinements are known only to us. Others know when we are limited by our circumstances, confined by an illness, or physically bound in a prison cell. And when people know, people watch. They want to see if what we say we believe is what they see us live out in seasons of confinement. As school children we were instructed to "wait, watch and listen" when nearing train crossings. This is exactly how others approach us when we are boxed in. Often they expect predictable behavior and are stymied by our responses. "How do you live with dialysis?" This is exactly what Peter is telling us —Be ready! For hope in the midst of suffering will trigger questions.

Tim Hansel, in his autobiographical book *You Gotta Keep Dancin'* comments: "Someone once asked a goldsmith how long he kept the gold in the fire. His reply, 'Until I see my face in it.' In his marvelous and mysterious way, God keeps shaping us until he can see Himself in our lives. The process is long, arduous, complex, and certainly not painless, but it's worth it." Ironically, hope in the heat of the refiner's fire will create a platform for our statement of trust that few other circumstances allow. What seems like utter foolishness is the ultimate demonstration of wisdom. It is both confounding and profound.

Watch for Opportunities

Watchfulness is the key to effective encouragement. I used to grimace at the phrase, "keeping my eyes peeled." I could envision bloody onion-like orbs. But comforters have their eyes wide open. There are two distinct pictures of watchfulness in scripture that describe the earthly conflict. We are told that our enemy "prowls around like a hungry, roaring lion, looking for some victim to tear apart." Christians are his A-List. If you have put your trust in Jesus Christ as your personal savior then you are a target for Satan's dinnertime. But there is another picture that brings us encouragement and boldness. "For the eyes of the Lord range throughout the earth to strengthen those whose hearts are fully committed to Him." Our enemy seeks to tear down; our Lord seeks to build up. Our eyes need to be constantly searching for the place where He would take us to minister His balm. We have the blessed opportunity of being ready to comfort with God's comfort. Where the enemy would plant discouragement we can plant the word of God that will undergird. We can stand in the gap for those who are confined for a season.

Encouragement By Choice

Winston laughed as he told me about his wife's substitute teaching in the local school district. "They have a new system so that you don't have the pressure of saying no to a 'real, live person.' The phone rings early in the morning. When she answers it she has the option of pushing #8 to accept or #9 to decline. She feels that the job is in her control and she doesn't have any interpersonal stress." The parallels were too good to ignore. How often God calls us to bring His encouragement, His comfort, His care or His exhortation; He gives us a choice. We can listen to that "still, small voice" and push #8 eagerly accepting His assignment. I was a huge fan of the series, Mission Impossible. I waited week by week for the next episode and for those now-famous words, "The task, if you choose to accept it…" But the last words were important, as well. "This tape will self-destruct in five seconds." Have you felt God's inklings in your spirit? Or how many times do we push #9 and roll over for a little bit more sleep? Have you chosen not to accept His assignment and then felt the opportunity self-destruct? There is no sweeter experience than being God's hands and feet! Let's practice pushing # 8.

Prepared For Action

Preparedness implies purposeful intent. Just as true encouragement that strengthens the heart is not haphazard nor random, true comfort is built on a foundation of readiness. Darlene always says that she is "paid up, prayed up and gassed up" so she is ready for God's work.

"Be prepared for what?" someone once asked Baden-Powell, the founder of Scouting. "Why, for any old thing," said Baden-Powell.

"His idea was that all Scouts should prepare themselves to become productive citizens and to give happiness to other people. He wanted each Scout to be ready in mind and body for any struggles, and to meet with a strong heart whatever challenges might lie ahead. Be prepared for life—to live happily and without regret, knowing that you have done your best. That's what the Scout motto means." (quoted from the Boy Scout Handbook)

In February of 2004 I took my Mom to the Dallas Theological Seminary's annual luncheon. How she enjoyed our day. As we were leaving the table my friend Lynda stopped us and said, "Let me take your picture." I hesitated but then hugged Mom's neck and smiled. A few weeks later a 11 x 14 print of this picture arrived. I don't care how healthy your self-esteem is, a closeup of your double chins is daunting. I put it away in my office and forgot it...until Mom died. Now it is framed and hanging in my office. She watches over me each day. After the memorial service I called Lynda to thank her for the picture that has become extremely dear. "I felt that God was telling me to take that picture. This will help me listen and respond more quickly the next time that I feel His prompting." Be prepared to be God's comfort!

Practice, Practice, Practice

Listening to His urgings is a practiced skill. Think of Abraham as he raised his hand to slaughter his son, Isaac. What if his mind had been so preoccupied that he hadn't heard the ram bleating in the bushes? Finely tuned spirits are the best spiritual antennas.

"May I speak to your Mommy?" "She is out in the backyard having her Jesus minutes, can you call back?" Carolyn Brakefield was my cherished Sunday School teacher in the Young Marrieds Class of First Baptist Church, Nashville. She and her husband, Jim, committed their lives to a group of 20-somethings who were venturing into parenthood, career, graduate school and just plain growing up. They saw our group through miscarriages, job changes, loss of parents, graduate dissertations, illnesses as well as sheer joys of pregnancy, promotions and delightful vacations. They were there whenever we needed them with a wise word from scripture and a loving hug. How did she access the comfort that was necessary for such a diverse class? She faithfully had her "Jesus minutes." To be a blessing we must be plugged into the blesser! The stoutest electrical cord lies lifeless unless it is connected to the power source. This means creating time to read His word and listen for His voice. He will give us abundant opportunities to do His work.

Watch and Pray

In the days of King Arthur magicians practiced alchemy—the science of turning lead into gold. Today we are just happy to make lemonade out of lemons, but the transformation of mourning into mornings of joy holds our attention. Even 50 years later I can picture the blue bottle which held the mysterious "eau de parfum" dramatically named Midnight in Paris. For a young girl this was exotic almost beyond imagination. Think of the mad life on the West Bank—and at midnight! Now another perfume fills my mind. This time it is the fragrance produced by my seasons of limitation. David rejoiced because God saved every tear and put it in a bottle. To me, the tears shed in divine confinement become a fragrant oil of offering. The aroma is more precious than Channel #5. Just as Jesus changed the water into wine at Cana He changes my tears into the sweet aroma of comfort. And as the host marveled that He saved the best for last I never cease to enjoy the divine desalination process that takes my salty weepings and converts them to drops of rare perfume. Your tears are in His bottle, as well. Pour them out in thanksgiving and anoint the lives of others. Watch for others who long for his aroma of comfort and celebrate the holy chemistry that remains a holy mystery.

Celebrate the Goodness of God

"I will tell the wondrous story when I lay my burdens down, 'Jesus led me all the way'"... Isn't that Israel's theme song? In Exodus 14:19-20 we read, "Then the Angel of God, who was leading the people of Israel, moved the cloud around behind them, and it stood between the people of Israel and the Egyptians. And that night, as it changed to a pillar of fire, it gave darkness to the Egyptians but light to the people of Israel! So the Egyptians couldn't find the Israelis!" (The Living Bible)

When we recognize the leading of God in our confinements it is a cause for celebration. Kenneth Caraway speaks poetically of "flattening the sides of the box and blowing off the top to make a dance floor on which to celebrate life." For me, life has to be spelled with a capital L for we are proclaiming the goodness of Him who came that we might have life, as the apostle John wrote in his account of Jesus. He is Life.

Ron Kerley spent years working with the homeless and hopeless. His description of them was "living in a cocoon." He worked in prisons and saw cell walls covered with pornography and cell walls covered with Bibles. "There was a strong correlation between what hung on the walls and what lived in their hearts," he said. With the message of a changed life through Jesus Christ he saw men and women emerge as butterflies who had lived wrapped in the brown shell of captivity. "It often takes awhile to overcome the hurts and the wounds, but when they heal it is time to say thanks!" Ron and his wife, Nancy, are spiritual entomologists who nurture the cocoon people and deliver glorious butterflies. As Richard Bach says, "what the caterpillar calls the end of the world the master calls a butterfly." In the most difficult days they are able to focus on the fact that "God is so good."

One Generation To Another

On a corner in Santa Fe sits an art gallery with a dramatic statue of three Indian women prominently displayed. On each trip to this intriguing New Mexico town I quickly hurry to make a prolonged visit to "the women." At first glance they look like they are standing together, wrapped in a blanket. But further investigation reveals that they are in fact standing on one another, wrapped in one blanket. This statue is reminiscent of the Indian fable that tells of the young woman who looks down and realizes that she is standing on the shoulders of an older woman. In shock she demands that the older woman take her place.

Despite the protests the older woman quietly responds, "Look down, my child." When the young woman extends her gaze she sees that the older woman is standing on the shoulders of another woman who is standing on the shoulders of an even older woman. The message is startlingly clear. We do not stand alone. We are wrapped in a blanket of fellowship and our feet are planted on the shoulders of those who came before us. When we step out into the sunshine that God will bring and we close the door behind us we are taking our position on the ladder of life. We have been comforted and now it is out turn to comfort. We have drunk deeply of His love and now we are to refresh others. We have taken hold of His grace and we are now to be gracious. As we look down we also look up to support the weight of those who are coming behind and we rejoice with Paul, "Thanks be to God for His indescribable gift."

REFLECTION

Getting A Foothold

1. When the season is over we need to close the door to take the next step.
2. Comforting others is a dividend paid on seasons of confinement.
3. True comfort, like true encouragement, is constructed on a foundation of preparedness.
4. God makes reapers out of weepers.

Gaining Ground

1. How do I know that the season is over?
2. What became or is becoming clearer during this time?
3. How can I face my confinement focused on making it count?
4. What does celebration look like for me?

REFLECTION

Following His Footsteps

Dear Father,_____

_____

_____

_____

_____

_____

_____

_____

_____

_____Amen

MUSINGS & AMUSINGS

"Faith, Hope and Love"

In heaven there will be no faith and hope because they are rooted in time. We trust that God will provide; we hope for future outcomes. In heaven it will all be clear and it will be unnecessary to look to tomorrow—it will all be today and knowable. But there will be love—all love, all the time. There will be worship, adoration and praise for those are timeless. "Faith, hope and love—but the greatest of these is love" because it is the only one that truly endures.

Father, while I am here on earth give me the grace to live by faith, live in hope and live out love. Father, in my times of confinement let me learn so that I am purposeful, prepared and practiced. Thank you for the boxes that you bring into my life to grow me into someone of usefulness. How I love You—I kick against You. Thank you for faithfully loving me, giving me Hope for tomorrow and assurance that it is in You, through You and for You.

MUSINGS & AMUSINGS

"Enjoy These Times"

"Enjoy these times, they'll be gone before you know it." How often I had heard that when my children were young. I gave them a weary half-smile in response. But "they" were right. Those days slipped by so quickly. Now I am the one saying that to frazzled young Moms in McDonald's. That emotion washed over me as I entered the restaurant and saw a Mother and Daughter engaged in conversation over lunch. Oh, it was hard not to break into their lives, "enjoy these times, they'll be gone before you know it." When did the fast forward button get pushed? How did days that crawled by begin an uncontrollable gallop? What did I learn that will help another daughter? Laugh a little louder, clean a little less, hug a lot more, forgive more quickly and say I love you over and over. One day I will find myself saying, "enjoy these times" without a tear's coming to my eye, but today I will just pause and thank the Lord for Mom.

FINAL WORDS

Colorado State University Tropical Meteorology Project predicted a 58% probability of a landfalling hurricane in Florida for 2004. We now know that Charley, Frances, Ivan and Jeanne did not read the memo on that report! As Texans we live in spring's "Tornado Alley." We all know the outline of the funnel cloud that arbitrarily touches down demolishing some and bypassing others. The Tsunami that devastated much of the Indian Ocean region swept aside property with abandon and crushed lives with casual indifference.

Hurricanes of Life

As we tracked 2004's historical hurricane season we could almost feel the dangerous breath on Florida's neck. Each report showed the exact location, the wind direction, the speed and the multiple variations of outcomes. We were mesmerized by the impending strikes and sat glued to the news networks as we watched reporters hanging on palm trees, fighting back 100 an hour winds. They certainly understood losing their footing. We followed the destruction and agonized over the loss of life. But we knew it was coming—the weather channel had done a countdown reminiscent of the "ball dropping" on New Year's Eve at Times Square. Unlike meteorological estimates we have a 100% probability of being hit by a major life storm that will limit our options. Some of our seasons have predictable landfall ranges because we know they are on the way and we know that we are in the path of a direct hit. For example, a degenerative illness that slowly, but systematically robs us of function; a nasty divorce that will go on for months of wrenching wrangling and legal maneuvering; or, the 5 year prison sentence to be served without possibility of parole. The winds are strong and we are often swept from our footing, but ordinarily the advanced warning system has given us some time to prepare by building up our support networks and bolstering our emotional reserves.

Tornado Times

In the mid-nineties I was gassing up the car in Eastern Nebraska. Next to me was a flatbed trailer loaded with intriguing machinery. Under Plexiglas domes were sophisticated dials, lenses, meters, lights

121

and gadgets. Although I am usually a solitary, non-gregarious gas pumper, this was just too fascinating to ignore. "How do you use that machine?" I asked. Expecting some technical response I was thoroughly surprised by his answer. "We are heading to Northern Iowa to find a tornado and film it for the movie, *Twister*. This is one of the camera units." Cool! These people were purposefully tracking tornado season and heading into maximum winds to capture Helen Hunt's dramatic whiplash. They knew exactly where touchdown was predicted. They knew precisely where to find maximum impact. They were choosing exposure to destruction. Some of our confinements are the result of bad choices. We overspend our credit cards; we choose "peace at any price" rather than standing up to our rebellious child; or we escape our dreary job by happy hours that get longer and longer. We are in a personal "tornado alley." At this point we are heading into the winds and will be like the drivers who are overtaken by tornadoes and cling to each other under highway underpasses. Tornadoes are fast-moving and often unpredictable, but they are also seasonal and regional. It is rare that bad choices and the emotional, relational, financial and spiritual confinements that result "just happen." Sometimes we ignore the warnings and drive directly into the path of destruction and suffer through serious confinements. Thankfully God's mercy and grace prevail when we fail. But the consequences, like ravaged property, are left as reminders of the tornado.

The Terror of Tsunamis

Other seasons are like the tsunami that strikes without warning, vacuums everyone into the undertow and then pulls them back out to sea. A sudden monster wave overtakes us and we are fighting for life. For example, a company merger leaves us without employment; a tragic car accident turns a Sunday drive into a lifetime of pain and disability; the discovery of drugs in our child's room shatters our dreams; the unexpected diagnosis of a debilitating disease instantly reprioritizes our decisions...these are tsunami events. We are strolling on the beach and without warning we are under the water! The early reports of the Asian tsunami described men and women standing outside a temple with their hands up as if helplessly fighting back the impending disaster. These Pompeiian moments capture the horror of sudden terror. Jack Nicklaus' grandson drowned in the family hot tub. In an interview the champion golfer commented, "We are grieving as we must. We will never get over this and we shouldn't. Our lives have been dramatically changed." Our comfort is in knowing that when God allows walls of water to rush against us He is still in control. The pain is profound and the grief is indescribable, but the season is superintended by a God who is there. C.S. Lewis calls pain "God's megaphone" for in these tsunamis of the soul God shouts to us.

Serving Others

Perhaps your season is defined by being the support team for another. The Red Cross lists "disaster care worker feeding" as one of its services. Bless you for your perseverance. Thank you for standing wordlessly with a loving heart. You are appreciated for those times when you don't know what to do, or what to say. But you are there. Maybe you are standing in the rubble of someone's life that you dearly love and are aching to know the outcome of their season. Are you standing in the gap? Are you holding up the arms of another in their time of confinement? You, too, will need firm footing. You will need wisdom, courage, strength and clarity. You will need the "joy of the Lord." My Dad has always quoted the line "He also serves you stands and waits." Your waiting is service to the Lord.

Next to my desk is a picture of my Mom taken when she was about my age. Her life was all about family. When we laughed, she did, too. When we cried, she was wracked with pain for us. When someone hurt us she was the grand dame of vindication. When someone loved us, she loved them even more. She was one who stood in the gap and assuredly held our arms through very hard seasons. When her oldest grandchild developed seizures and temporary paralysis she drove 12 hours non-stop to be at the hospital. When a grandson was hospitalized after a car accident no one could stop her as she headed for the emergency room. Even in her failing health she made her way to Presbyterian Hospital to hold her youngest great-grandchild and kiss her granddaughter. She was a true encourager whose life was about serving.

She entered into the seasons of our lives with a passion rarely seen. Her engagement with us was finally rewarded as we certainly did rise up and call her blessed. But we gave her a run for her money during the early years when she was at home with three strong-willed, determined children. She experienced her own confinement and limitation as she chose to forego career to fulfill her dreams of being a wife and mother.

Later in life Parkinson's disease created a series of limitations for her that were excruciating. No more driving, no more shopping, no more "taking care of" and finally no more speaking. Her season of disability was painful for all of us, but we knew that it was our time to care for her. We had traded places, but she was always the Mom that never changed. With her last words she wanted to bless us. Our hardest seasons may be ahead but the lessons that we learned from Mom will enable us to keep our feet from stumbling. I have learned to depend on God because there really is no better choice; to acknowledge the reality of where I am because nothing happens until I get honest; to embrace God's grace and deny perfectionism no matter how good it looks; to ask for help from those who are truly helpful and with God's strength to comfort others in their own confinements.

Benediction

Whether you are struggling to keep from sliding down the hill or you are extending a hand to another, my prayer is that your eyes will be on Him. "For of Him and through Him and to Him are all things to whom be glory forever. Amen" (Romans 11:36–New International Version)

Thank you for traveling with me as we have seen that confinement coming through God's hand is divine. I hope that you have stopped along the road to review your own life story. Remember, that your boxed-in times are not over. As long as you live you will experience limitations, but the lessons that we learn will give us greater traction and stability for future slippery slopes. The Five Footholds are not a formula, nor are they the final word. They are the principles that have helped me and hopefully will be useful to you. Please keep sight of the truth that life may not be fair, but the Lord God Almighty is in control. Life may bring hurt and pain and question marks, but He is available and His grace avails. Seeing His hand in each season gives us the power to "never lose the good of a bad situation." And perhaps most importantly, we are to be comforted and then to comfort others. Our lives are to be a thank offering to our most holy God.

Our journey has come to an end. Through these pages He has woven us together. How much I have enjoyed walking with you. The Lord has blessed me so greatly as I pictured you, prayed for you and constantly gave thanks for your life. May you stand firm in the faith, prepared and alert. And may your seasons of limitation be gloriously received as Divine Confinement.

A Word "Just Between Us"

As you have read I am confidant that your own story has come to mind. Treasure your own journey. See how God has prepared you and lovingly guided you. And then when you want to, please share your story with me. I have a website designed just to hear from you. Tell me of the lessons that you have learned in your own divine confinement. Write to me of the slippery slopes that you have navigated. I really want your life to be part of the continuing journal of men and women who know what the hand of God in limitation is about. We are a community of faith and therefore share in the joys and sorrows of one another.

Talk to me at www.divineconfinement.com

"Maybe nothing is more important than that we keep track, you and I, of these stories of who we are and where we have come from and the people we have met along the way because it is precisely through these stories in all their particularity, as I have long believed and, often said, that God makes Himself known to each of us most powerfully and personally."

"If this is true, it means that to lose track of our stories is to be profoundly impoverished not only humanly but also spiritually."

Frederick Buechner, excerpted from "Telling Secrets"

Recommendations for Further Reading:

Hendricks, William, *The Light That Never Dies*, Northfield Publications, Chicago, 2005

Lindbergh, Anne Morrow, *Gift From The Sea*, Pantheon Books, New York, 1955

Graham, Ruth Bell, *Footprints of a Pilgrim*, Word Publishing, Nashville, 2001

Swenson, Richard A., MD, *Margin*, NavPress, Colorado Springs, 1992

Briscoe, Jill, *There's A Snake In My Garden*, The Zondervan Corporation, Grand Rapids, 1975

Barg, Gary, *The Fearless Caregiver*, Caregiver Media Group, Herndon, VA, 2001

Bagnull, Marlene, *My Turn To Care*, Thomas Nelson Publishers, Nashville, 1994

Thomas, W. Ian, *The Saving Life of Christ*, Zondervan Publishing House, Grand Rapids, 1961

Thomas, W. Ian, *The Mystery of Godliness*, Zondervan Publishing House, Grand Rapids, 1964

Yancey, Philip, *Where Is God When It Hurts*, Zondervan Publishing House, Grand Rapids, 1977

Winebrenner, Jan, *The Grace of Catastrophe*, Moody Publishers, Chicago, 2005

Spurgeon, Charles Haddon, *Letters of Charles Haddon Spurgeon*, The Banner of Truth Trust, Carlisle, PA., 1992

Smith, Fred, *You and Your Network*, Executive Books, Harrisburg, PA, 1984

Tournier, Paul, *To Understand Each Other*, John Knox Press, Atlanta, 1962

Mayhall, Carole, *Lord Of My Rocking Boat*, NavPress, Colorado Springs, 1981

Myra, Harold, *Is There A Place I Can Scream?*, Tyndale House Publishers, Wheaton, 1979

Pink, Arthur W., *The Attributes of God*, Baker Book House, Grand Rapids, 1975

Lucado, Max, *Safe in the Shepherd's Arms*, J. Countryman, Nashville, 2002

Packer, J.I., *Keep In Step With The Spirit*, Fleming H. Revell, Old Tappan, New Jersey, 1984

Piper, John, *The Misery of Job and The Mercy of God*, Crossway Books, Wheaton, 2002

Chambers, Oswald, *My Utmost For His Highest*, Dodd, Mead & Company, Inc., New York, 1935

Jones, Charlie, *Life Is Tremendous*, Executive Books, Mechanicsburg, Pennsylvania, 1988

Arthur G. Bennett (Editor), *Valley of Vision: A Collection of Puritan Prayers and Devotions*, Banner of Truth Press, Carlisle, Pennsylvania, 2003